Being Muslim on Campus

Being Muslim on Campus

Religion, Inclusion, and Agency at a Secular University

ABIYA AHMED

OXFORD
UNIVERSITY PRESS

OXFORD
UNIVERSITY PRESS

Oxford University Press is a department of the University of Oxford.
It furthers the University's objective of excellence in research, scholarship,
and education by publishing worldwide. Oxford is a registered trade mark of
Oxford University Press in the UK and in certain other countries.

Published in the United States of America by Oxford University Press
546 Fifth Avenue, New York, NY 10036, United States of America.

Library of Congress Cataloging-in-Publication Data
Names: Ahmed, Abiya author
Title: Being Muslim on campus : religion, inclusion, and agency at a secular university / Abiya Ahmed.
Description: New York : Oxford University Press, [2026] |
Includes bibliographical references and index.
Identifiers: LCCN 2026007487 (print) | LCCN 2026007488 (ebook) |
ISBN 9780197773598 paperback | ISBN 9780197773581 hardback |
ISBN 9780197773628 online | ISBN 9780197773611 epub
Subjects: LCSH: College students—Religious life—United States | Muslim college students—United States | Education, Higher—United States | Multicultural education—United States | Multiculturalism—United States
Classification: LCC BL625.9.C64 A46 2026 (print) | LCC BL625.9.C64 (ebook)
LC record available at https://lccn.loc.gov/2026007487
LC ebook record available at https://lccn.loc.gov/2026007488

DOI: 10.1093/9780197773628.001.0001

Paperback printed by Integrated Books International, United States of America
Hardback printed by Lightning Source, Inc., United States of America

MIX
Paper
FSC FSC® C183721

The manufacturer's authorized representative in the EU for product safety is
Oxford University Press España S.A. of Parque Empresarial San Fernando de Henares,
Avenida de Castilla, 2 – 28830 Madrid (www.oup.es/en or product.safety@oup.com).
OUP España S.A. also acts as importer into Spain of products made by the manufacturer.

Contents

Preface

In my role as a student affairs professional at Stanford, I often get requests from colleagues to advise or mediate on students' issues and accommodations, especially those related to Muslim or Muslim-adjacent students. Once, colleagues from another unit reached out to meet regarding a student who could not attend their scheduled mandatory training because the timing coincided with the last few days of Ramadan and the celebration of Eid. The email indicated that my colleagues were being flexible and that they simply wanted to consult. I met with them, and they reassured me that they had given this student options: she could attend parts of the training if it suited her schedule, or she could simply review the content at a later time.

Since the accommodation had already been made, I was a little unclear about the purpose of the meeting and expressed as much to my colleagues. They shared feedback from the student which, somewhat to my surprise and, I must admit, also to my delight, was a sharp critique of scheduling the mandated trainings during Ramadan and Eid in the first place. In particular, the student had noted the dual burden of educating administrators regarding why Ramadan and Eid were special Muslim days and therefore a reason for the conflict, and then of determining a later time to undergo the training while missing out on the crucial opportunity to do so with peers. She had also pointed out that these trainings would have never been scheduled during Christmas.

My colleagues agreed that the student had made some valid points, but they were unsure about how to address the critique. To their credit, they had taken the time to reach out and consult me; however, I was finding myself paralyzed not by a loss of words but by having too many. Ultimately, I suggested they validate the student's concerns and perhaps plan differently in future. I also reassured them that, in my estimation, the student's critique was an indictment of systems and not of any particular staff member. There is much more I would have liked to say, but in a half-hour meeting, how could I address decades of Protestant Christian religious hegemony in the United States, the persistence of that hegemony in the guise of secularity, the role of the academy in perpetuating this hegemony via supposed neutrality, which then results in institutional policies and decisions—including but certainly not limited to calendaring—that ultimately led to a case such as this one?

For that kind of exposition, I would have to write a book. This is that book.

My curiosity about the Muslim college experience is what led me to conduct research for this book. I grew up in the United Arab Emirates, where I went to school from kindergarten to undergrad. My own college experience, therefore, was markedly different from that of Muslim students here with respect to engaging Islam and Muslimness (though of course it was also very similar in other typical college-going ways). When we were growing up, religion was a thing for us, but it was never *the* thing. This might have been a feature of my family's parenting philosophy or of the Muslim-majority context I was in, or both. So, when I moved to the United States twenty years ago, I quickly realized that religion, or race, or gender, was often *the* thing. Identity markers, especially minority ones—due to internal consciousness or via the external gaze—were central in both discourse and lived experience, and I had better learn how to navigate that.

That learning curve led me to questions about how Muslim college students negotiate their religious commitments in secular college settings. In this equation, I had taken for granted the fluidity of religious commitments and the neutrality of secularity. I had assumed that while in college the students would make specific moves vis-à-vis their Muslim beliefs and commitments, and it was *this* side of the equation that I would essentially interrogate. I wasn't entirely wrong, and that is indeed where I began. But the more I spoke with and observed the students, the more I realized that the other side of the equation—that is, secularity—also warranted interrogation. The students I spent time with weren't simply inhabiting "secular" spaces and structures that were objective vis-à-vis religions and religious commitments. The secularity they experienced, in fact, did privilege specific ideas about religion and specific ways of being religious, which then impacted the kinds of moves they made with respect to their own Muslim commitments. The students enacted and acted upon their Islam and Muslimness, but their institution and its secularity also acted upon them and intervened in this process.

So, while I began with the students, and they continue to be the main actors in this book, what they ultimately helped unearth is not just how they negotiate their commitments but also how their campus triggers and mediates those negotiations. Where I end up, then, is using the case of Muslim students to question how higher education can treat institutional secularity as an impartial, equal-opportunity arbiter of faith and religious commitments. It is not.

And then there is this: my own journey of having been primarily a researcher of these issues to also becoming a practitioner. I am now an institutional agent myself and am likely complicit in a similar institutional mediation process, embodying those contradictions. In some ways, this is the epitome of irony. In other ways, it is a full-circle moment and an opportunity to offer some corrective to what my interlocutors experienced and taught me, and what students continue to teach me every day.

Introduction

In this book, I will tell three stories. The first story is about the secular not being secular: how institutions claiming secularity, and, through secularity, purported neutrality on religion, in fact privilege Protestant Christian[1] notions of religion and religiosity. The second story is about inclusion attempts that fall short: how institutional diversity work, in part because it does not consider the first story, ends up limiting and becoming challenging for those meant to be included. The last story is about students being sharp, creative agents: how they *are* aware of the first two stories because they experience them and how *they* challenge secularity even as it is challenging for them.

At one private and residential "secular" campus in the United States—Bellington University (BU)[2]—I spent almost three years (2017–2020) doing fieldwork, participant observation, and interviews with Muslim students. This book details their experiences and negotiation of Muslimness at their campus and over the course of their undergraduate career. While I share several anecdotes and incidents, at its core, this is a book about three stories that intersect in the experiences of my interlocutors at BU.

The case of Muslim students at BU is specific, but these stories are universal. BU is part of a larger higher education context where the place of religion must be understood simultaneously with the role of secularization. Writing in the mid-1990s, historians like George Marsden considered secularization of the academy to be an all-encompassing process that shut religion out;[3] more recently, however, higher education experts like Jacobsen and Jacobsen and

Being Muslim on Campus. Abiya Ahmed, Oxford University Press. © Oxford University Press 2026.
DOI: 10.1093/9780197773628.003.0001

Schmaulzbauer and Mahoney have argued that religion does, indeed, have a place on campus because higher education now exists in a "postsecular" age.[4] The latter perspective also contends that religion on campus not only survives but also often thrives, continuing to contribute to diversity and pluralism.[5]

Does it thrive, though? And, if so, what does this thriving look like? The case of Muslim students at BU adds texture to and interrogates these standard narratives of religion in higher education. As these Muslim students are immersed in what appears to them a secular institution, they encounter religion generally and engage Islam specifically via Protestant features, which expect Religion (with a capital "R") to be individual, textual, private, and separate from politics and law.[6] These Protestant framings of religion, which also then inform secularity's framing of religion, trickle down to BU students as they experience being Muslim and as they seek to understand and grapple with Islam. In doing so, they express confusion, exercise agency, and embody resistance in their own ways.

Their case compels us to consider *which* ideas of religion and *what kind of* religious pluralism thrives on campus and the discursive structures that make this selective thriving possible. It tells us how institutional structures privilege particular ways of knowing and being, and how an institution's pervasive ideological apparatus allows it to recruit minorities and their religious difference to maintain and further its own secular pluralist image. It also shows us how, for some religious communities, the place of religion on campus remains fraught in subtle but significant ways.

Religion at a Secular Campus: Hidden in Plain Sight

If we are to interrogate the place of religion on campus, why go looking for it at a secular university? Bender and Taves have shown that religion is "entangled" not just conceptually but also institutionally with multiple other features of modernity, especially secularity.[7] While scholars have begun to theoretically reconceptualize religion and secularity, methodologically the study of religion remains situated primarily within sites and spaces that are considered overtly religious. However, as Cadge and Konieczny observe, "there is much to learn about religion through the study of its presence in secular organizations, precisely because it is 'hidden in plain sight.'" They explain how "making 'invisible religion' visible" within secular social contexts such as airports, fire departments, hospitals, prisons, and colleges and universities helps elucidate "how individuals piece together a *bricolage* of meanings, including those forged from religious beliefs and practice" and helps inform "the past and present trajectory of American religion" more broadly.[8]

In the context of higher education specifically, scholars like Marsden[9] and Sommerville[10] contend that American higher education is wholly secular and characterized by "established nonbelief." More recently, Jacobsen and Jacobsen and Schmaulzbauer and Mahoney have challenged that perspective to argue that religion on campus is, in fact, "no longer invisible."[11] However, such discourses assume a normative definition of religion rooted in the Protestant sense of the term. Jacobsen and Jacobsen, for example, acknowledge the difficulty of defining religion, but eventually they revert to its usage as a singular category characterized by Paul Tillich's rendering of it as "ultimate concern."[12] They also do not consider diverse student voices in their treatment of religion, which would likely complicate how religion is typically understood.

Thus, my purpose in electing to research religion at a secular institution is not just to make the "invisible" visible but to also interrogate what is already visible vis-à-vis religion and secularity, and how that impacts the "bricolage of meanings" that individuals piece together. In this book, these individuals are Muslim students, who come from a religious tradition that is not only not Protestant but also one in which the religious and the secular often coalesce in different ways.[13] Exploring their embedded experience in a university context that is considered secular thus sharpens the focus on what kind of religion is "hidden in plain sight" and what kind of religion has no place in plain sight.

False Secularity and Fragile Inclusion

Returning for a moment, then, to the first of the stories of this book, in Chapter 1 ("Protestant Secularity"), I take a deep dive into the concept of the secular, the process of secularization, and its intersection with higher education and the academy. It is the only heavily theoretical and historical chapter, and the journey is worthwhile.

Just in case, however, here is the gist of the chapter: religious and secular studies scholars have long established that the categories of religion and secularity have a Protestant Christian genealogy and that Protestant influences on these categories continue to endure, even if they are not obvious.[14] This has implications for higher education, and particularly for non-Protestant students—Muslims, but also many others—who assume that their campus context is secular but find that characterization confusing as they live out their own religious beliefs and commitments. This is because many academic institutions, despite their complicity in the secularization process, perpetuate and operate on the assumption that secularity is religion-neutral, when in fact it privileges specific Protestant Christian notions of religion.[15] For these reasons, I propose it is more accurate to characterize a secular campus context as "Protestant–secular,"[16] acknowledging the persistence and entanglement of Protestant Christianity with secularity. This is the essence of the first story.

The second story on inclusion efforts takes center stage in Chapter 2 ("Pluralism on Protestant Terms"), and I pull on its threads throughout the book. What I want to do next is not offer you the short version but rather situate this inclusion story in the current political moment—a moment when diversity and inclusion work especially within higher education is under strict scrutiny and attack.

When I was conducting my research, between 2017 and 2020, we were in the first Trump wave where the rise of Christian nationalism became closely associated with anti-Muslim sentiment and Islamophobia.[17] Donald Trump's 2016 election and the subsequent shock and outrage it engendered among some would seem to indicate that his ascendancy to power—and, by extension, the wielding of white Christian privilege—was the exception and not the rule of America's legacy. As a response to this wave, progressives doubled down on diversity, and additional efforts were made (and not just on college campuses) to make sure Muslims were "included" and were made to feel like they belonged.

However, as Jonathan Rosa and Yarimar Bonilla have argued, Trump's election should be considered an impeachment of liberal democracy and not an exception to it, making evident the contradictions inherent within it.[18] Indeed, on the cusp of the November 2024 elections, we were back to where we started: Trump was once again on the ballot running against a woman, though this time a woman of color in the form of Kamala Harris. His return only affirmed the conclusion that Trump and Trumpism were as American as apple pie. And while Harris's candidacy certainly mobilized the political left more so than Joe Biden's incumbency, it was also fraught with acute disapproval and distance from liberals due to her position on the ongoing war in Gaza.[19] But marginalized communities have for a long time contested political formations that lead to such moments. Such longstanding resistance, Rosa and Bonilla note, should compel us to pursue "new alternatives that seek to decolonize liberal institutions, rather than simply 'diversifying' them" because performative diversity work that does not locate racial logics and power dynamics in colonial systems ends up harming those made most vulnerable.[20]

In this vein, and in the aftermath of the Gaza War and the ensuing pro-Palestinian advocacy and campus protests in

2023–2024, diversity, equity, and inclusion (DEI) efforts have also come under attack.[21] The criticism, however, is not that they need to more seriously foreground "decoloniality" per Rosa and Bonilla above. Rather, political conservatives, latching onto the rise of anti-Palestinian bias, Islamophobia, and antisemitism, have seen an opportunity to undermine diversity work and seized it.[22]

To the extent that diversity efforts have surged without sufficient consideration of the frameworks that inform and contain them and of how much they truly serve religiously marginalized or minoritized populations, they are certainly not beyond critique.[23] We can find one such critique in Evelyn Alsultany's book *Broken: The Failed Promise of Muslim Inclusion*, which compellingly demonstrates the benefits and pitfalls of what she calls "crisis diversity": a mode of temporarily enacting diversity initiatives to include Muslims when high-profile Islamophobic incidents or policies take place, only to ignore them until the next crisis happens.[24] Even when crisis diversity occurs, however, she illustrates—using the University of Michigan as a case study—that DEI efforts fall short when it comes to the issue of Palestine and advocacy for Palestinians. Alsultany's work predates the 2023–2024 pro-Palestinian campus advocacy, but her contention that one clear limitation of DEI on college campuses is Palestine engagement has only been affirmed by recent institutional responses to student protests and campus activism.[25] The scale and scope of student activism and expression both nationally and internationally, along with the subsequent institutional and federal responses, will surely generate more books, but this is not one of them.

Pluralism and DEI

This book is about *another* limitation of inclusion efforts with respect to Muslim students: institutional secularity. More specifically, the limitation is a result of insufficient consideration for the pervasiveness of the Protestant–secular institutional context.

To be sure, higher education *has* accommodated and included, albeit imperfectly, minority religious students under various frameworks and systems ranging from multiculturalism to interfaith to pluralism to DEI. In revealing the limitation of these inclusion efforts, however, I am not suggesting that current DEI frameworks be replaced wholesale with some version of pluralism, a move that has gained traction recently. As I discuss below and more in depth in Chapter 2, pluralism can sometimes be even more problematic than DEI because it seeks to engage difference without accounting for historical inequalities that have led to current power configurations among various groups.

Pluralism's contribution to the diversity project of higher education, especially vis-à-vis religious minority students, lies in the fact that it has what Amanda Porterfield has called a "pro-religion bias."[26] In this way and especially if contrasted with conventionally understood secularity (as antireligion or neutral), pluralism acknowledges that religions and religious communities are a net positive and of some value to the world. At first blush, then, it would seem to be the inevitable framework to apply within college campuses when considering inclusion of religious minorities such as Muslims. Pluralism, however, does not sufficiently contend with its own history and the conditions under which inclusion is made possible. Notwithstanding the captivation with American idealism in works of scholars and practitioners such as Danielle Allen and Eboo Patel, campus pluralism, as Shabana Mir has shown in her book *Muslim Women on Campus*, allows only a "limited range of difference" in that, in order to be celebrated or included, Muslim students must adhere to a certain set of expected practices.[27]

This is not the only issue, however. For my analysis, the core problem is that pluralism brushes aside issues of power and privilege, inevitably neglecting the fact that whoever builds the "inclusion container," so to speak, gets to decide the parameters of inclusion and, indeed, of containment. As I discuss at length in Chapter 2, pluralism's pro-religion bias is, in fact, a pro-Protestant Christianity bias. This means that even when the framework is applied in an apparently secular context, *because the secular is not actually secular*, the terms of inclusion end up being dictated by Protestant Christianity.

Meanwhile, DEI's contribution to the higher education diversity project—at least theoretically and somewhat practically—has been that it has, in fact, foregrounded historical power and privilege vis-à-vis race, gender, and, to some extent, class.[28] Moreover, it *has* served Muslim students because it has accounted for them at times as a racialized minority and at other times as a politically marginalized minority in the wake of events such as 9/11 and the Muslim Ban. What it has not done for Muslims is sufficiently account for their differentiated religiosity and religious ways of being or knowing, relative to white liberal Protestant Christianity. In this way it has manifested the same problem as pluralism, that is, the limitations of inclusion, though for different reasons.

My contention is that DEI frameworks have been applied in contexts considered "secular" without a sufficient interrogation of the secular and the pervasive power dynamics at play there. This position might seem contrary to DEI's philosophical underpinnings, because DEI *has* taken into consideration structural inequalities, power imbalances, and to some extent, decoloniality, vis-à-vis race, class, and gender. This is the very basis of DEI initiatives, especially in higher education and even more so after the murder of George Floyd in 2020.[29] So why not apply the same philosophical analyses of power to religion and religious minorities?

If we were to take seriously the prevalent critiques of DEI, it would be easy to conclude that one reason DEI has not effectively served religious minority students is that religion has either been excluded or has been an afterthought in DEI work.[30] Notably, critiques perpetuate the myth that because DEI theory and praxis construe everything in terms of identity (and, more specifically racial identity),[31] religious identity can be configured into the DEI framework only if it intersects in some way with other identity markers on the matrix, or, as one critic, disputing the coding of Islamophobia as racism, put it, "Religious bigotry sits on the lap of racism instead of having its own seat at the table of intersecting hierarchies."[32]

It is true that identity politics can sometimes take center stage in some DEI work and that both an overemphasis on identity and a performative nod to it can sometimes compromise the nuances of diversity work. However, an obsession with altogether dismantling identity as a feature of diversity and inclusion is not only unpragmatic, it also obscures the fact that what is really at play here is the consideration of power and privilege.

I would posit that the main reason DEI has not deconstructed religious hegemonies is that the form and function of secularity have, until very recently, remained uncontested and largely unexplored in the higher education discourse on diversity. A thorough exposition of DEI and its critiques is beyond the scope of this book, but I want to reiterate this point: my central thesis is that institutions and institutional officers have failed to seriously consider Protestant–secular formations of how college campuses treat categories of religion and secularity, which ultimately impact the diversity and inclusion work they do. At the heart of this argument are the power and privilege that Protestant Christianity wields in the guise of secularity, and thus, by extension, in how campuses interact with religion and minority religious students—in this case Muslim students. This failure, then, is not meant to be a blanket indictment of DEI. Rather, it calls attention to the fact that the analytical lens that DEI applies to other categories (race, gender, class) *also needs to be applied to religion.* In future, the work of diversity, equity, and inclusion may be defined in other terms,[33] but insofar as considerations of power, privilege, and structural inequalities continue to remain a defining feature of the work, the case of BU Muslim students substantiates the need for more of this work, not less.

Muslim Students as Critiques

In using the case of BU Muslim students and their experiences as a critique of both the categories of religion and secularity, and institutional reproduction of those categories, I depart slightly from the typical treatment of Muslim students found in the research conducted on or with them. Such research has helped further our understanding of individual or small groups of Muslim students on campus. However, it stops short of critically analyzing the normative categories, paradigms, and power structures that ultimately create conditions in which Muslim students, as a matter of necessity, must negotiate their Muslimness and Islam. Through the experiences of BU Muslim students, we can learn more about such negotiation, but I also use those experiences and discourses to critique institutional framings of religion and secularity in general and of Muslimness and Islam in particular.

Barring notable exceptions and a general resurgence of interest in Muslim students after the pro-Palestinian advocacy and campus protests of 2023–2024, much of the research on Muslim students, conducted mostly in the post-9/11 context, has typically focused either on elements of Muslim students' identity formation or on institutional accommodations. Some examples of these works include Lori Peek's seminal paper on the identity development of second-generation Muslim Americans after 9/11;[34] Nasir and Al-Amin's description of institutional factors impacting Muslim students' sense of safe identities and belonging on campus;[35] Shafiqa Ahamdi's and Darnell Cole's work on Patriot Act, surveillance, and Islamophobia impacting Muslim students;[36] and Ahmed et al.'s examination of the correlation between risk factors and religiosity among Muslim students.[37]

These strands of research focus on Muslim students' minority status and the influence of broader sociopolitical climate vis-à-vis Islam and Muslims. What we learn from this literature is that in addition to the myriad challenges college students face as part of their emerging adulthood,[38] the experience of Muslims on campus is mediated by factors such as personal religious practice and related needs as well as broader political issues such as Islamophobia, otherizing, and the pressure to conform.

These factors converge in Shabana Mir's ethnographic study on Muslim women undergraduates, perhaps the most detailed work thus far of the Muslim campus experience, focused on gender.[39] Mir examines how these students are burdened with responding to social pressures within a "hedonistic" campus culture. Her research offers insight into what these students perceive as "normal" on campus, for they find it difficult to navigate through three unifiers of campus social life: alcohol, attire, and dating. She illustrates how these students struggle to construct authentic identities, either compromising on religious principles or feeling denied social access. Campus pluralism, she argues, accepts a "limited range of difference," which implies that religious Muslim women are considered "normal" only through "concealed religiosity." If they engage in drinking or dating or in taking off their *hijab*, for instance, they are celebrated. Thus, liberal pluralism in American higher education, she writes, "both falters and succeeds."[40] Mir's work is important to consider because it departs from other research not only in its methodology but also in its extended analysis and implications. When read closely, Mir's analysis of Muslim women undergraduates is also a critique of dominant paradigms such as liberal pluralism, while highlighting the "agency and strategy of the marginalized."[41]

In this book, I build on Mir's work in two ways. First, I ask and aim to answer the question: what has changed for Muslims students since her research? Mir collected her data primarily between 2002 and 2003, immediately post-9/11 and at the height of the War on Terror. Two decades later, it would make sense to ask if Muslim students face the same issues as they did then in terms of religious identity and whether the needle has moved at all. I argue that it has moved, in that issues such as dating, drinking, or attire are not the primary sites of these Muslim students' struggles. This is not necessarily because campus culture has changed, but because the discourse of pluralism and DEI has led institutions like BU to accommodate more intentionally—and often to celebrate—religious identity and practice. For Muslim students, this has meant more spatial and ritual accommodations that have made it easier for them to practice Islam on campus in some ways. This is certainly true not only for many private and well-resourced campuses, but also for many public campuses. At the same time, Muslim students do face other challenges having primarily to do with what religious ideas and beliefs are allowed in campus discourse.

Second, I build on Mir's work by presenting the case of Muslim students as a critique not just of liberal pluralism, but also of dominant paradigms pertaining to religion and secularity. These paradigms assume that religion and secularity are universal categories in which groups such as Muslims can easily fit or be made to fit. As the experience of BU Muslim students will show, this is not the case for them. Moreover, I argue that their experiences interrogate the standard narratives of the place of religion in higher education, which assume that religion in American higher education is, on one hand, either completely absent and shut out[42] or, on the other, that it survives and thrives.[43] The case of BU Muslim students reveals a third possibility: *that some ideas about religion survive and thrive, while others are kept hidden*. Moreover, as I focus on institutional factors and how they impact the Muslim experience on campus, I also highlight the agency, autonomy, and authenticity of these students in curating their experience on campus to be able to live out their Muslimness and Islam in ways that make sense for them.

Bellington University

Bellington University (BU), a relatively small, private institution in the United States, houses both undergraduates and graduates on and around campus. I have anonymized the campus to protect the confidentiality and identities of my interlocutors. However, situating it among other higher educational institutions and understanding its history in parallel with theirs will help clarify the campus context.

Marsden has extensively documented the fact that while institutions like Harvard, Yale, and Princeton began as explicitly Christian colleges for the purpose of training clergy, universities like Cornell and the University of Chicago were positioned as nonsectarian "modern" responses to those institutions. However, as Marsden also illustrates through founding documents and statements, even nonsectarian institutions have a Protestant Christian establishment history. Andrew White and Ezra Cornell, for example, continually emphasized that Cornell would be a nonsectarian institution but a Christian one nevertheless, with high moral values and uninhibited scientific inquiry. Similarly, through the statements of William Harper and Jane Stanford, Marsden shows how the University of Chicago and Stanford University, respectively, were institutions that championed nondenominationalism while situating the pursuit of knowledge and the primacy of reason and science as inherently Protestant values. Such framing was common among American universities and would leave "indelible marks" on them.[44] Their roots, writes Marsden, cannot be understood as having anything other than a Protestant heritage. Bellington University is one such campus, whose establishment has a Protestant history and continues to exhibit Protestant features in its secularity.

In terms of students' religious affiliation, data on the 2016 incoming undergraduate class revealed that almost a quarter of the students identified as "None," followed by Roman Catholic, atheists, and Protestant. Smaller groups included Mormons, Jews, Hindus, Buddhists, and Muslims. Data on the religious affiliation of graduate students was unavailable at the time of this writing.[45] Since it is a residential institution, most students live on or around campus, even if they are local to the area. The university's residential character implies that students operate in a limited context away from their families. They form new social networks and are highly integrated into the university's culture. Because of this immersive nature, even though Muslim students form a small group of the overall student population, they have been able to carve out spaces for themselves on campus.

BU has a Religious Life Office (RLO) that houses a Muslim chaplain and offers space for Friday prayer and congregation. The RLO has its roots in the campus's church. Like many universities founded in the eighteenth and nineteenth centuries that had a chapel or church at the center of campus, BU, too, has a church on campus. However, unlike other campuses at the time, church attendance was not compulsory. Based on archival data, BU was progressive for its time in terms of religious inclusion, as the university's church was nondenominational but decidedly Protestant. In addition, the founders were known to welcome people of all and no religions. Still, the church's and its clergy's primary orientation remained Protestant Christianity well into the twentieth century, reflected in their decisions to bar worship services conducted in other faiths (including Catholicism).

This changed in the 1960s and 1970s when a new leadership was able to institute sectarian worship service and changed even more so in the 1990s after the hiring of Jewish and Muslim clergy. In the following decades, the unit grew in terms not only of religious and gender diversity but also physical space. Today, its staff and services continue to be at the church often, but they are also placed in the student center on campus, which also has worship spaces and services for students of different faiths. Chaplains from various religionsincluding Jewish and Muslim—also have their offices there. During my research, RLO and BU's Muslim chaplain at the time played important roles in the lives of the students I shadowed and interviewed.

In addition, there is a vibrant Muslim Student Association (MSA) at BU, run primarily by students. The founding of Muslim Student

Associations (MSA) in American higher education coincides with the rise of postmodernism, the civil rights movement, and the influx of immigrants from Muslim countries in the 1960s in the wake of the 1965 Immigration Act. The first MSA was founded in 1963 at the University of Illinois at Urbana-Champaign, and there are now more than five hundred chapters across the United States and Canada.[46] Based on archival data, the BU Muslim student community, like its counterparts at many peer institutions across the country, had organized itself in the 1950 and 1960s and founded the MSA. Throughout the twentieth century, it underwent multiple iterations, resulting in name changes and offshoot groups. Today, the BU MSA is the official student-run Muslim organization on campus, which helps oversees both spiritual and social activities. Additionally, the university also regularly offers *halal* food options on campus.

BU also has a Mosaic Cultural Center (MCC), which is dedicated hub for social, academic, cultural, and wellness resources on the SSWANA (South Asian, Southwest Asian, Middle Eastern, and North African) regions and on broader Muslim-related issues. The creation of this center follows the trajectory of community and multicultural centers being established at American campuses, which began in the 1960s after the civil rights movement. These centers foster belonging for students of minority communities, also aiding in retention and graduation, while also supporting their institutional mission and serving the larger campus community.[47] In this vein, the MCC was also created as a resource and space to bridge the gap between community and curriculum, working alongside various campus partners to offer deep insight into local and global Muslim contexts, and supporting diverse students, faculty, staff, and alumni.

Participants

I first started conducting exploratory fieldwork at BU in September 2016 as a participant observer. From September 2016 until June

2017, I made periodic visits to the campus to familiarize myself with the campus context and the Muslim students. Sometimes I would attend the Friday prayer services; other times I would attend events hosted by the MCC or the MSA. Based on these observations and my informal interactions with students, I selected eight students to be my key interlocutors for the remainder of my data collection. Between July 2017 and September 2019, I continued to attend events on campus but focused my observations and fieldwork to spend more time with these eight students. In addition to almost thirty in-depth interviews with these eight students, I also had over fifty casual conversations with them as well as other students. I had fortunately completed my fieldwork before the campus shutdown due to the COVID-19 pandemic, but I did conduct additional interviews with my key interlocutors after that, concluding them in June 2020.

I selected the following eight students based on my initial observations of them as interesting interlocutors and because they represent racial, gender, and class diversity within the Muslim student population. They also represent the transnational experience of many young American Muslims. When I selected them, all were sophomores except for Ayesha, who was in her first year. By the time I finished my data collection, they were all seniors (and Ayesha a junior). I describe them briefly below. While I have altered some details slightly to protect their identities, essential characteristics have been preserved to illustrate the diversity of the group.

- **Yusuf**: Turkish American, upper middle class. Yusuf was born and raised on the West Coast.
- **Kareem**: Egyptian American, first-generation/low-income, on financial aid. Kareem was born in Egypt but moved to America when he was two and was raised on the East Coast.
- **Khalil**: African American, lower middle class. Khalil was born and raised in the American South, identified himself as a descendant of African slaves, and associated strongly with Imam Warith Deen's community.

- **Amira**: Malaysian American, upper-middle class. Amira was born and raised on the West Coast.
- **Ayesha**: Pakistani American, upper-middle class. Ayesha was born in the Midwest and was raised mostly in the United States.
- **Idris**: Ethiopian American, first-generation/low-income, on financial aid. Idris was born and raised on the East Coast.
- **Zara**: Indian American, middle class. Zara was born on the East Coast, grew up in the Middle East and South Asia. Zara moved to the United States permanently after she began her studies at BU.
- **Amani**: Tanzanian American, middle class. Amani was born on the West Coast, raised in the Middle East. Amani visited the United States every summer and moved permanently to the US after joining BU.

Analytical Lenses

Let me add a brief note about my methodological orientation and analytical lens. I wanted to understand the students' experience at various scales: in their personal and day-to-day lives, in their immediate and intimate friend groups and/or communities, and also in the institution at large. In order to do so, I found most helpful Omer Lizardo's modes of culture (declarative, nondeclarative, and public)[48] and Rinaldo and Guhin's[49] mapping of data collection methods onto these three modes. Briefly, declarative culture can be articulated via language (saying), whereas nondeclarative culture is more embodied (doing). Both are personal elements of culture in that they are "contained within a person." At the same time, there is a public culture "out there" that interacts with these personal modes to produce the totality of an individual's experience. In this book, I have aimed to access all of these elements (personal and public) to better understand the Muslim students' experience on campus.

I used ethnographic interviews, participant observation, and think-aloud exercises with the students to gather data and learn from them. In particular, I found that a combination of participation observation and ethnographic interviews helped unlock another type of cultural mode that Rinaldo and Guhin call "meso-level public culture." As they observe:

> This meso-level is only accessible after the sociologist has gained sufficient "local knowledge" (Geertz 2008) to understand meso-level cultural forms in both the declarative and nondeclarative modes, everything from shared mottos and aphorisms to the Bourdiesian doxa only visible to a critical hermeneutics.[50]

I found this form of analytical mapping helpful in describing what I have aimed to accomplish: applying methodologies that would make multiple levels of analysis accessible to me: macro (at the institutional level), micro (at the individual level), as well as meso (at the community level). Moreover, by combining interviews and participation observations (in various forms), I have aimed to access both the declarative and nondeclarative cultural modes of these Muslim students' experience on campus, as well as the role of institutional public culture in mediating these experiences.

With regard to the conceptual framework that guides my analysis, I describe the theoretical framing in the next chapter, but I want to note here an important point about my analytical lens. Islam, like many other religions, especially in America, is a "religio-racial" formation. Judith Weisenfeld has used the term *religio-racial* "to designate a set of early twentieth-century black religious movements whose members believed that understanding black people's true racial history and identity revealed their correct and divinely ordained religious orientation."[51] For the groups in her book, race and religion are entangled and cannot be understood apart from each other. Her analysis is helpful for understanding the experience of other racial and religious identities, including

Muslims in present-day America. In other words, race and religion co-constitute the experience of Muslims in America across all racial and ethnic categories and religious denominations.[52] While I do not employ an overt racial analysis per se to the experience of Muslim students at their campus, I am attuned to the fact that Muslim experience in America is always already a religio-racial one. Race, therefore, is ever present in this book not just in the form of the racial diversity of my participants but also in the experience of these students on campus as both religious *and* racial minorities, and ultimately in the critique of dominant paradigms of religion and secularity that are rooted in white Protestant Christianity.

Chapter Overview

In Chapter 1 ("Protestant–Secularity"), I offer a historical and theoretical overview of secularity and religion, their relationship with Protestantism in America, and how that impacts the place of religion in higher education broadly. I draw on concepts and considerations from the discipline of religious studies and apply them to higher education: that modern secularity has a Protestant tinge at least or is wholly Protestant at most is not news to religious studies scholars.[53] This observation, however, is not considered in the higher education context when one is determining institutional initiatives vis-à-vis religious minority communities. Thus, my goal in this chapter is to take you on a short theoretical and historical journey that illustrates the Protestant historical roots and influences on secularity and religion in the United States and the endurance of such influences in contemporary times. Our journey ends with my proposal that the operative campus context of many "secular" institutions generally, and of BU particularly, should be more appropriately termed "Protestant–secular."

This theoretical culmination becomes the point of departure for subsequent chapters, which empirically illustrate how the application of a "Protestant–secular" lens to the BU context brings into sharper focus the challenges of being Muslim at a secular campus and reveals the institutional blind spots when addressing those challenges. Chapter 2 ("Pluralism's Power") dives into the Protestant roots of pluralism, an inclusion framework that is resurging after the 2023–2024 campus activism. Within this framework, BU offers various institutional accommodations for Muslim students and marks certain Islamic celebrations such as Ramadan, Eid, and the Prophet Muhammad's birthday. How Muslim students view and engage with these accommodations and celebrations is illustrative of how BU propagates a Protestant version of pluralism and diversity. Their perspectives also show us how religious pluralism on campus serves the institution more than it serves them. From a macro- to a meso-level approach, in Chapter 3 ("Privatization in Public") I explore how specific notions that reify religion and a liberal/conservative discursive structure rooted in Protestant–secular logics lead Muslim students at BU to keep their own religious beliefs, ideas, and questions private. I do this by examining intracommunity campus discourses on gender and Islam, which are a robust site for how these tensions play out. These discourses fall short of offering constructive spaces to Muslim students for examining their perspectives by limiting their choices to a liberal/conservative binary. Given this limitation, students privatize their religious beliefs and ideas. I argue thus that even as these campus discourses make visible a particular notion of religion, the students' own ideas about Islam and religion remain invisible. In Chapter 4 ("Personalization of Faith"), we move to a micro analytical approach to sharpen the focus on Muslim students' lived experience. In this chapter, we see these students exercise creative agency and personal authenticity so that they can engage Islam and Muslimness on their own terms; despite being embedded in an institution whose Protestant–secular context limits the set of possibilities for them. Characterizing this process as their personalization of faith, I argue that these students live and embody contradictions, showing us that there is a different way to do diversity and inclusion work if we take our students seriously, considering them as agents and not as objects of this work. Finally, in Chapter 5 I offer some closing thoughts and recommendations for future work and research in the "Conclusion."

1
Both/And: Higher Education and the Making of "Protestant–Secularity"

One winter afternoon in 2018, during a full day of interviews and fieldwork at Bellington University (BU), I decided to take a break. I walked toward the designated Muslim prayer room, which is a small space located in one of the campus student center buildings. On my previous visits, I had found it usually empty except for the occasional student. With new navy-blue prayer rugs and plush green cushions, the room was a cozy enough spot where I could relax for a short while before heading to my next commitment.

When I entered the room, I was the only one there. But not long after I had put down my backpack and settled, I heard the door open. I looked up and saw a familiar face. It was Zara, an Indian American sophomore and economics major, whom I had known since her first year at BU. She had since become an invaluable interlocutor for me, offering critical insights for my research.

"Assalaamualaykum!" she said to me with a smile, as she put her backpack down.

"Walaykumassalam," I replied, "How are you?"

"Ugh, it's been a crazy day, and I only just found time to pray *dhuhr* (the noon prayer), I better get to it before the time ends!" It was almost time for the late afternoon prayer (which would indicate the end of the time frame for the noon prayer), so I nodded quickly, and she proceeded to pray. I sat silently until she finished within a few minutes. Then, after raising her hands to her face to

Being Muslim on Campus. Abiya Ahmed, Oxford University Press. © Oxford University Press 2026.
DOI: 10.1093/9780197773628.003.0002

make a quick supplication, she turned to me, "How are you, Abiya? Sorry I just wanted to finish praying first before saying anything."

"Of course. I'm well, thanks. It's been a busy day for me too, I thought I'd just take a break before my next interview."

"How's the research going? Can you tell us what you're finding out?" Zara asked me.

I smiled and told her it was still early on in my data collection, and it would be difficult for me to offer any conclusions just yet. She nodded, "Well, I think it's great you're researching this stuff. We don't really discuss religion here, I mean except with you, and you're a researcher, not a student." I could sense my "break" turning into more "data collection" as Zara kept going, unprompted. "It's very, very strange—like this place [Bellington University] is secular but just secular by name. But actually, it's so religious."

"Yeah? How do you figure that?"

"Well, I've met so many people here who are closeted religious people. Almost everyone."

"You mean Muslims?"

"Everyone, but Muslims especially are scared to come out of the closet. So, it's harder to get them to talk about it, if they have decided to maintain the 'secular' image," she explained, emphasizing air quotes around the term "secular" with her hands. "They can't even admit that '*Well, actually we are religious, we're just not bringing it up*.' With other people, Christians especially, which is the predominant religion, even if they pretend to not be religious, it's still easier to bring in religious belief or practice if they want to." She kept talking as she stood up, put on her backpack, fixed her floral red *hijab*, and started to open the door. "For Muslims it's just harder I think, and so yeah . . . I've met a lot of religious people here, but people just don't talk about it. It's no big deal though. Anyway, I gotta run, I have a class across campus!" I saw her slip into her Nikes and run out as the door closed.

With that, Zara was gone, leaving me to think about everything she had said. Her spontaneous remarks on religion, secularity, and

Muslims at her campus were at the crux of my research, and she had made them so casually before walking out, almost as an afterthought. She had remarked that "it was no big deal," but it obviously was *somewhat* of a big deal to her. Zara and I would inevitably follow up on this conversation; but, at that moment, knowing that she rarely minced her words, I wondered why she felt she had to temper her discourse on religion with her peers or generally on campus. As I was to later discover, Zara was not alone in feeling this way: many Muslim students expressed uneasiness with having conversations about religion on campus. This was surprising, given that BU champions diversity and pluralism, including religious pluralism. Zara and I had that conversation in a room designated for Muslims to perform their prayers, which itself is part of a larger dedicated space for various religious events and observations, including the Friday congregational prayer. So, clearly there was some institutional accommodation for Muslim students. But evidently there was also something about the institution's secular environment that was challenging for Muslim students, even if they thought it was "no big deal," as Zara had said.

Right after Zara left, I made some quick notes on a page that I titled "BU: Secular or Not???" This chapter tackles that question through a historical and theoretical journey in which we engage with literature and concepts from Religious Studies and intersect them with higher education. In the first section, I provide a conceptual overview of how scholars have treated the categories of secularity and religion, and I examine why prevalent terminology fails to accommodate the experience of religion for all religious groups. Moving away from abstraction, in the second section I offer a more focused overview of secularity in the American context. Finally, in the third section, I describe the history of religion and secularity specifically in higher education and show how the academy has contributed to the production of the categories of religion and secularity in ways that privilege a particular understanding of religion and marginalize others.

Secularity

There is no dearth of writing on all things associated with "the secular," but because terminology surrounding the discourse on the secular can be confusing, an appropriate point of departure is Jose Casanova's essay *The Secular and Secularisms.*[1] Casanova describes the distinctions between "the secular," "secularization," and "secularism" as follows:

- "the secular" is an epistemic category that creates and codifies a realm *differentiated* from "the religious";
- "secularization" is a process describing the transformation and differentiation of "the religious" and "the secular" from early modern to contemporary societies;
- "secularism" is a modern knowledge regime or doxa that can manifest itself as ideology or statecraft.

In distinguishing between secularism as ideology and as statecraft, Casanova writes that the latter is meant to serve as guiding principle or policy for the separation of religious and political authority for the purpose of neutrality and/or equality. However, building on Talal Asad's treatise on how secularism reifies religion as a specific category,[2] Casanova contends that "secularism becomes an ideology the moment it entails a theory of what 'religion' is or does."[3] Casanova himself is more concerned with phenomenological secularism, especially as a taken-for-granted reality for ordinary people.

In this regard, Charles Taylor's approach to secularity is also helpful, especially in terms of how he disaggregates it.[4] He contends that secularity can be understood in three primary terms: (1) as a public realm free of God: this does not mean that God cannot configure in people's private lives, but rather that economic, political, professional, recreational, cultural, and educational realms, among others, operate on principles that do not include God; (2) as a decline of religiosity: that is, a general turn away from God and institutionalized religion in the form of church attendance, for example; and (3) as altered conditions of belief: by this Taylor means that there has been a shift from belief in God or faith being the norm to it becoming one option among many and an "embattled" one in Christian society. In other words, the altered condition of belief is that "belief in God is no longer axiomatic."[5] Taylor is more interested in addressing secularity in this third sense, which, according to him, is the "phenomenological experience that constitutes our age paradigmatically as a secular one, irrespective of the extent to which people living in this age may still hold religious or theistic beliefs."[6]

The key takeaway from Taylor's framing is that regardless of individual relationships with religion and God, the characteristic feature of our time is secularity in the sense that there is an aversion to or an avoidance of transcendence / God, encapsulated in what Taylor calls the "immanent frame."[7] Casanova calls this "the naturalization of 'unbelief' or 'nonreligion' as the normal human condition," and he couples that with the contradiction that there are secular modern societies (such as the United States) that appear to operate within the immanent frame Taylor proposes but whose populations are "conspicuously religious" or involved in some sort of religious revival.[8] That religions continue to play a public role is an argument that Casanova had originally made in *Public Religions in the Modern World*,[9] in which he asserted that secularization as differentiation was the only tenable thesis, showing empirically that the other two elements of secularization—privatization and decline of religion—were actually not modern structural trends.

In analyzing the context of my interlocutors—Muslim students at BU—my central focus is phenomenological secularism and its role in mediating religion for ordinary lives in a specific institutional context. Taylor's and Casanova's framings are thus relevant for both terminological and conceptual reasons. First, I adopt Casanova's distinctions between the secular, secularization, and secularism. Because "secularization" is a process that refers to a historical (and linear) trajectory of the secular "overcoming" the religious, it is not my primary focus, and I use that term sparingly. The primary terms for my purpose, then, are "secularism" or "secularity," which I use interchangeably.[10] In addition, when I use these terms, I do not mean political secularism, as Saba Mahmood has discussed,[11] or secularism as a statecraft principle or secularism as it relates to market forces.[12] Instead, I am referring to secularity as doxa or a knowledge regime that constructs and guides the context in which Muslim students on campus negotiate their religion and religious commitments.

This brings me to the conceptual takeaway, which is that the phenomenological secularism or the immanent frame that Taylor refers to is also *ideological* in the sense that secularity *does* take a position vis-à-vis religion. By this I do not mean that there is a state established religion, as that would explicitly counter the church/state separation claimed by secularism. I am also not referring to the ideological position as one in which secularism is adversarial to religion. Although that is not an uncommon understanding of secularity, I agree with Mahmood that one of the fundamental contributions of Taylor's magnum opus is the "authoritative dismantling of the idea that religion and secularism are antithetical worldviews, forever locked in an epistemological battle. . . ."[13]

By ideological secularism, then, I mean that the position of secularity is *not* religion-neutral. I construe that lack of neutrality in terms of the production of religion as a category as well as the Protestant influence on secularity, which are two sides of the same coin. More strongly, to produce the category of "religion" is to reproduce Protestant notions of it or, in other words, secularity is not religion-neutral because it has a Protestant bias. This Protestant bias is key, and I discuss it further in the next section on secularity in the American context.

Before that, however, let me say a few words about the term "religion." Without delving too much into the etymological and historical issues associated with defining the term, I do want to emphasize two critical points. First, as J. Z. Smith,[14] Asad,[15] and several others[16] have noted, our context is one in which we have moved from "religions" (plural) to "religion" (singular), creating a universal category out of it. This is a double-edged sword because "the category of universal religion can simultaneously allow that all humans are alike in their propensity toward religion *and* serve to differentiate among humans on the basis of their different religions."[17] That universality, then, is imposed in the sense that individual religions are measured against features that are, in fact, particular to a dominant understanding of religion.

That leads me to the second point about the challenge of the term "religion": it implies a collective experience, but it inevitably means different things to different people. That paradox is at the heart of the tension that BU students face, as we will see in later chapters. As Brent Nongbri has noted, leveraging Wittgenstein, "the meaning of a word is its use in the language."[18] For this reason, Nongbri defines religion as "anything that resembles Protestant Christianity," a definition that he admits is "crass, simplistic, ethnocentric, Christianocentric, and even a bit flippant, but also highly accurate in reflecting the uses of the term in modern languages."[19] I agree, and for my purpose, this tactic is also progressive in that it moves forward my analysis without getting too caught up in semantics. In this way, I adopt an approach similar to that proposed by Mutakkabir and Nuriddin, whose work on religious minority students in higher education is built upon deploying a functionalist definition of religion, which highlights its role in power dynamics among various groups.[20] When I use the term "religion," then, I imply the category with all its historical and Protestant-centric connotations of "being private, voluntary, individual, textual, and believed . . ." which, as Winnifred Sullivan explains, has come to be considered as true religion (or religion with a capital "R"). She goes on to note that "public, coercive, communal, oral, and enacted religion on the other hand, was seen to be false." Sullivan contends that the second kind of religion (with a lowercase "r") has been historically represented by Roman Catholicism, exists in the form of Islam today, and is also the religion of most people.[21] The implications of the term, then, are really important for Muslim students as they try to negotiate their religious commitments in a secular context, particularly because their religious commitments do not fit the normative definitions of religion qua Protestant Christianity.[22]

Secularity in the American Context

Let's turn next to the other side of the coin, namely, the Protestant influence on secularity. Given that the category of religion is modeled after Protestantism, the idea that secularity too would incur Protestant influence is unsurprising even if paradoxical. With respect to Charles Taylor's work, Warner, VanAntwerpen, and Calhoun note, "at the center of Taylor's account is an epic irony: that secularity in its modern Western sense is significantly a product of the long history of reform movements within Western Christianity" and of Protestantism in particular.[23] This means that our "conditions of belief," though presumably secular, inevitably have Protestant features. Thus far I have elaborated on this paradox theoretically, but it is worthwhile also to briefly examine it specifically in the American context. In doing so, I focus on three scholars—John Modern, Tracy Fessenden, and Amanda Porterfield—whose works have been generative for the discourse on religion and secularity in the American context. Exploring their works briefly will help cement the Protestant influence on secularity (and religion) in America and ultimately lead us to question what this means for other groups, such as Muslims.

In *Secularism in Antebellum America*, John Modern explores the Protestant genealogy of secularism through eclectic data sources. His book is disciplinarily vast with several important points, two of which are especially noteworthy for our purposes. First, Modern identifies a particular strand of evangelicalism that became popular in mid-nineteenth century America, one that emphasized individual choice and agency over external authority, allowing religion to be "grounded deep within the self."[24] This emphasis on individual freedom and a plethora of religious (and nonreligious) choices that is now so ubiquitous in American society can also be understood in terms of Taylor's[25] conditions of belief or Peter Berger's "plausibility structure,"[26] which essentially allude to the circumstances (networks, social contexts, environments) that make individual beliefs possible. Modern's chronicling of secularity in antebellum America establishes the roots of these circumstances in evangelicalism. Second, Modern's work on "evangelical secularism" also brings into focus the paradox of pluralism: as he chronicles in his examination of Bible societies and the evangelical obsession with technology and new media, the imperative toward mass dissemination was also motivated by the need to make public the value and authenticity of evangelicalism as true religion. So, one hand, there was the drive toward individual freedom and choice and, on the other, "evangelical secularism helped set the terms that all arguments about religion had to adopt in order to become intelligible."[27]

Closely related to Modern's work is Fessenden's *Culture and Redemption*. Her work is important in no small part because she coined the very term "Protestant–secular" and, in her book, she presents the paradox of secularity posing as universal while actually being particular.[28] Through a close reading of American texts from the *New England Primer* to *The Great Gatsby*, she shows us how Protestant ideologies normatively persist in American culture in the guise of secularity. Whether it is the 1870 court decision declaring the King James Bible as nonsectarian or redemption via Protestantism in *Uncle Tom's Cabin*, Fessenden illustrates how these (and other) classic American moves and motifs are indicative of a "Protestant–secular continuum" to which all things non-Protestant must adapt. As she writes, "to consider the career of secularization in American culture is therefore also necessarily to consider the consolidation of a Protestant ideology that has grown more entrenched and controlling even as its manifestations have often become less visibly religious."[29] Like Modern's work, *Culture and Redemption* also raises the question of the limits of pluralism, given the unspoken imperative to ultimately conform to a Protestant model of religion even with acknowledgment of difference.

In this regard, and especially with respect to pluralism, Amanda Porterfield's work on *The Transformation of American Religion* is also relevant.[30] She outlines several trends in American religion during the late twentieth century, including the ecumenism that came with the Reformed Protestant tradition, the collapse of traditional religious authority, and an emphasis on individualism, among others. Each of these trends, as she carefully documents, has roots in American Puritanism, and they are reflected in the fact that "Protestant attitudes, ideas, and principles" endure and shape how we think about American religion. Porterfield's work is a critical intellectual history of American religious thought and part of the story of secularity in the American context. It is especially relevant when one is considering how Protestantism continues to mediate how we think about pluralism. Her own personal account of encountering Eastern religions is insightful: "There was something about Zen that was new and freshly vital, but it was my *Protestant orientation* to the world that led me to this discovery" (emphasis mine).[31] This viewpoint is noteworthy not because we must place a valence on Porterfield's (or anyone's) "Protestant orientation to the world," but because such an orientation is so central to secularity and religion in the United States, regardless of one's affiliation with or affinity to Protestantism. Inevitably, then, given its Gramscian hegemony, we must ask—if the story of religion and secularity in the American context is riddled with Protestantism in many ways, what does that mean for non-Protestants in the United States?

Secularity, Religion, and Higher Education

That question is a broad one and can be explored in a number of ways. This book aims to tackle it in the context of higher education by investigating the case of Muslim students at a secular campus. In the previous chapter, I situated Bellington University among comparable institutions and discussed all the ways in which examining religion at a university, in particular BU, can make visible what is hidden in plain sight. Here, I present a more in-depth story of religion and secularity in higher education so that we can contextualize that history and better situate the present moment.

In the following sections, I discuss higher education's religious origins, followed by more insight into the context of secularity and the secularization process, and finally the postsecular era that presumably indicates a reengagement of religion in higher education. The key takeaway of this journey is to challenge conventional narratives on religion, secularity, and higher education, which often reinforce the religious/secular binary, the linear trajectory of secularization, and present secularity as something that happened *to* the university. In fact, as Tomoko Masuzawa has argued in *The Invention of World Religions*, the academy is complicit in producing secularity:

> Academic secularity cannot be thought to be a natural *pre*condition for the mission of the institution devoted to scientific inquiry or its *after*effect; rather, the academy as we know it has been deeply entangled in the production of the secular, in a relationship that is at once instrumental and symbiotic.[32]

Throughout this history of religion and secularity in the academy, institutions have made willful moves to treat religion and secularity in ways that are convenient and beneficial for them. In the early history ("Origins"), this convenience is reflected in attempts to preserve the Protestant influence by imagining progress, scientific inquiry, and moral prowess as inherently Protestant values. In a later time period after the twentieth century ("Secularity"), the academy's complicity in producing secularity is evident in the production of the Religious Studies discipline and the validation of religious identity via the identity politics discourse, while relegating religion to extracurriculars. Finally, in the present day ("Postsecularity"), when religion is said to have made a more forceful "comeback" to higher education, the academy continues to reproduce Protestant notions of religion while presenting secularity as being religion-neutral.

Origins

The religious and particularly Protestant roots of American higher education are well documented, as is the modern and secular turn.[33] Until the late 1800s, American higher education was not only mostly Protestant, it was also elitist. Most students were white and male, and college presidents were often ordained Protestant clergy who taught a course on moral values and theology rooted in Protestant Christianity in the service of American ideals.[34] As Jacobsen and Jacobsen note, "going to college was a kind of finishing school for future Protestant leaders in a Protestant America." They call this era of higher education the "Protestant era," a time when academia was characterized by clergy training and mandating courses in Christianity.[35] Soon, however, other religiously and denominationally affiliated colleges—such as Georgetown University, founded in 1798—also sprang up across the country.

In the late 1800s, explicit Protestant influence in higher education began to decline. Some accounts consider this decline not necessarily motivated by antireligious prejudice but as an inevitable outcome of "educational modernization" whereby a focus on technical skills, scientific facts, and methods of inquiry naturally meant there was little room for theology.[36] A key catalyst in this process was the

Morrill Land Grant of 1862 (and later 1890), which allowed for the building of institutions with the explicit mission of responding to the Industrial Revolution and focusing on science and engineering (as opposed to liberal arts). This shift, however, did not mean that Christianity was completely sidelined. But even when other religious denominational groups as well as Black and Indigenous people of color were admitted, those in charge of educating did so under the pretext of "saving the other."[37] As Marsden illustrates using the case of Cornell (one of the few remaining private land-grant institutions), "university building in the late nineteenth century was part and parcel of the victorious Republicans' efforts to harness American technological potential," all of which was "part of a single Protestant hope to uplift humanity."[38]

Other scholars frame the shift as part of an explicit "secular revolution," such that secularization of American institutions was not an inevitable byproduct of modernization but a willful one. As Christian Smith argues, the elimination of religion from American institutions (including higher education) was an intentional movement concerned fundamentally with questions of power and authority. According to Smith, conventional secularization theory is problematic because, among other things, it takes away human agency and does not pay close attention to relational, structural, and economic factors. He instead frames the process of secularization through the language of revolutionary movements, whereby a group of people with specific interests had grievances against established religious power, which motivated them to actively disrupt the status quo. Particularly in the case of higher education, Smith argues that factors central to the secular revolution included (1) the rise of academic elites seeking to establish themselves as secular authorities; (2) educational reformers who were often in leadership positions, such as college presidents, and their approaches; and (3) the professionalization of university faculty seeking to become a "class for itself." This revolution, he writes, "transformed higher education from college institutions promoting a general

Protestant worldview and morality into universities where religious concerns were marginalized in favor of the 'objective' a-religious, and irreligious pursuit and transmission of knowledge and credentialing of new professions."[39] Smith's framing of the changes in higher education as a "secular revolution" illustrates the complicity of institutions and academics in producing secularity on campus.

In addition, Marsden's account adds texture to Smith's account by noting the role Christian (and specifically Protestant) intellectuals and college administrators played in the process. Put differently, Smith adds the element of human agency in the secularization process, and Marsden attributes that agency specifically to Protestant college presidents and faculty. As he explains, liberal theologians especially championed liberalism, nonsectarianism, and moral and scientific progress because they considered morality and not theology to be central to salvation.[40] That "earthly" pursuits were embedded in Christian practice was not an innovation. As Porterfield illustrates, an older iteration of this idea can be found in Augustine's *The City of God*, which influenced reform movements in challenging religious hierarchy and promoting the idea that ordinary Christians living their worldly lives were equally eligible for salvation and God's grace. Thus, "for Protestant reformers, the secular world was the locus of Christian practice and the domain where they hoped to see the sovereign will of God become manifest."[41] The impetus to "secularize" higher education, therefore, was rooted in liberal Christian (Protestant) beliefs about the place of religion and religious people in the world.

Secularity

By the start of the twentieth century, American higher education—once an explicitly Christian enterprise—was transforming such that a secular paradigmatic approach to knowledge and inquiry was taking precedence, brushing aside religion to extracurriculars such as chapel services and baccalaureate prayers.[42] In this way, religion could still play a small part in colleges and universities but stay out of meaningful discourse and inquiry, a process that Marsden terms "methodological secularization." As he writes, "pious Christians were expected to leave their religious beliefs at the door, even if they had prayed to God to bless their work and came from their discoveries praising God for his work."[43] Methodological secularization can be further understood in terms of two separate but related strands: the development of Religious Studies as a discipline and the legitimization of religious identity as part of identity politics.

Religious Studies

The first strand—the development of the Religious Studies discipline—illustrates a shift from teaching religion to teaching *about* religion. In this book I am primarily concerned with Muslim students' lived experience outside of class, so I do not explore Muslim students' interfacing with Religious Studies classes at their campus. However, it is important still to know the context of Religious Studies because it contributes to the phenomenological secularity of the institution in which these students are situated. Moreover, if we look at the development of the Religious Studies discipline in the academy as a case study, we can see how the academy is complicit in producing secularity.[44]

At first, the simultaneous secularization of higher education and the rise of Religious Studies departments appear to be inconsistent, but only if we discount the role these departments had in advancing secularity in higher education. As Schmalzbauer and Mahoney note and many others have pointed out similarly, "while often portrayed as secular, the field of Religious Studies is the cultural and institutional offspring of liberal Protestantism."[45] In other words, because the secularization process was facilitated by liberal Protestantism,[46] one consequence of this was making religion an academic object of study.

The "creation story" of Religious Studies is often traced back to the 1963 Supreme Court case *Abington Township v. Schempp*, in which the Court ruled that public schools may not require students to read Bible verses and recite the Lord's Prayer as this requirement violated the First Amendment's Establishment Clause. The decision affirmed that schools cannot endorse specific religious practices and must remain neutral—or "academic"—on religion. This decision is often seen as critical to the development of Religious Studies as a scholarly discipline. However, Sarah Imhoff illustrates how the flourishing of Religious Studies predates that decision, which grounds that process firmly in the earlier years of the Cold War. Part of it was that student interest in religion had increased as a way to make sense of turbulent times.[47] Primarily, however, what made it possible was the influx of federal funding. By "following the money," Russell McCutcheon[48] has also shown that Cold War politics and funding from sources such as the National Defense Fund (NDF) and the Danforth Foundation led to the invention of Religious Studies. Liberal scholars, he explains, utilized Cold War rhetoric and the perceived Soviet threat to "make-over" theology and divinity degrees and to legitimize the study of religion as a branch of the humanities. The Religious Studies discipline, he concludes, is a legacy of "disillusioned liberal Protestant scholars who, although no longer part of a comfortable hegemony, nonetheless possessed sufficient cunning intelligence to take full advantage of a brief but significant window of opportunity to create a new field and a host of new jobs, and along the way, set the agenda that would shape the discipline for the coming generations."[49] Imhoff builds on McCutcheon's exploratory research to also conclude that "universities participated in and capitalized on cultural notions of American religiosity and Cold War rhetoric," which contributed to the flourishing of Religious Studies.[50] Moreover, because Religious

Studies had the baggage of overt Protestant establishments and seminaries, it was perceived as a "second-class discipline," and, therefore, additional and intentional efforts were made to make it more scientific and acceptable to the academy.[51] In other words, the Religious Studies discipline was not an organic byproduct of the "secularization" of higher education. Rather, its creation was willful and expedient while furthering the production of secularity in the academy, which ultimately had Protestant underpinnings that continue to endure.

Relatedly, a key feature of Religious Studies departments was "world religions." This, too, is a Christian legacy. In *The Invention of World Religions*, Tomoko Masuzawa has documented that the concept of "world religions," while seemingly inclusive and pluralistic, actually preserves Christian exceptionalism.[52] The comparative religion approach and the inclusion of other religions as objects of study was a move that Christian theologians made to highlight differences between "pseudo-religions" and Christianity as the true religion. The best illustration of this is her chapter on comparative theologians who, in their willingness to include other religions worth studying, came up with the essence of what true religion is or should be, which allowed them to categorize other religions as incomplete versions that could only approximate Christianity. I mention this here to illustrate not only the lasting Christian influence on what counts as religion, but also to note how "world religions" continues to be a feature of Religious Studies departments on campus.

The academic study of religion, thus, would inevitably flourish simultaneously with secularization of higher education in post-World War II America.[53] This does not mean, however, that it was definitively secular. The *Schempp* decision has certainly been used to justify it as secular, as faculty drew a clear distinction between religious scholarship and religious belief. However, like other aspects of the secularization process, one might argue that the approach and methodology of Religious Studies in many ways also indicates the triumph of liberal Protestantism.[54]

Religious Identity (vs. Religious Beliefs)

The second strand—the legitimization of religious identity as part of identity politics on campus —is also an important feature of the secularization story because it, too, illustrates how universities managed to reproduce Protestant notions of religion and secularity.

Robert Wuthnow has pointed out that two significant trends that emerged in the 1960s and gained traction in the 1970s and 1980s would become central to the story of religion and higher education: postmodernism and the civil rights movement.[55] The latter resulted in identity politics activism, particularly with respect to justice along racial and gender lines. For higher education, this meant student campus activism, but it also led to the creation of academic departments, programs, and community centers that catered to minority populations such as African Americans and Asian Americans, and to women. The university was no longer dominantly white, male, and Protestant (in its composition at least; less so perhaps in its leadership). In addition, the postmodernist orientation led to epistemological debates about ways of knowing in various fields in the sciences, social sciences, and humanities. This context for understanding the resurgence of religion in higher education is important because, as Wuthnow writes:

> The epistemological uncertainty, not to mention the dynamic campus politics that accompanied it, did create opportunities for rethinking the place of faith in the academy. If it was now legitimate to be African American or gay, and to argue that there were special ways of knowing that might come from emphasizing one's racial tradition or approaching literature through the lens

> of queer theory, it also became more legitimate to be Catholic or Jewish or Presbyterian. . . ."[56]

In other words, identity politics made it possible to connect identity with epistemology, but for religious identity, "exactly *how* it was legitimate was of course unclear . . ."[57] Part of that legitimacy was to validate Religious Studies programs or campus religious groups, which, in structural ways, continued to reinforce Protestant notions of religion and secularity. So, for example, Religious Studies classes would address the historical development and cultural influences of religions, but not necessarily challenge students to consider or channel their religious beliefs. Campus student activism would serve to protect religious identities but not necessarily welcome religious beliefs into discourse. The epistemological implication of this stance is the paradoxical messaging that religion was both similar to and different from race and gender or other forms of identity. On one hand, it was similar because a religious identity (other than Protestant) was now acceptable on campus just like diverse racial and gender identities. On the other hand, it was different because unlike the (now widespread) acknowledgment that theoretical frameworks can have authentic grounding in gender or racial orientations (e.g., feminist theory or Afrocentric epistemology), religion cannot be an epistemological source in a secular setting.[58] As Wuthnow writes, "Religion and faith commitments have largely become matters of cultural tradition and have ceased being about truth." For him, this implies that religion will continue to stay on the margins in the academy.[59]

For my purpose, if we juxtapose this reality with the larger context of secularity and religion in American higher education, it becomes evident how keeping religion and faith separate from questions of "truth" reinforces Protestant notions of religion, particularly the notion that religion should be individual and private. This, to use Warren Nord's phrase, has been the "liberal solution to the religion problem"[60]: granting religion-free disciplinary and academic autonomy to scholars while allowing religion to stay on the margins of campus life through supporting religious student groups, such as the Muslim Student Association or affiliated community spaces. To be sure, the liberal approach to religion includes an acknowledgment that students should be taught *something* about religion and faith and spirituality. For example, the American Academy of Religion (AAR) issued "Religious Literacy Guidelines" for American universities and colleges, noting that "every college graduate ought to have a basic understanding of religion as a part of human experience."[61] However, what this understanding entails, or how it might be taught, or to what extent it benefits students remains elusive. As it was in the postwar era,[62] contemporary research on religion and spirituality in higher education and young adult development has confirmed that there is still student interest in "ultimate questions" and the exploration of faith, characteristic of emerging adulthood.[63] However, as Gorski et al. have noted, social sciences have had to bracket questions of personal religious truths in order to analyze more "observable" and "verifiable" dimensions of religion, such as rituals and communities. To do so, other dimensions, such as religious belief and personal experiences of faith had to be considered irrational and subjective, and therefore unanalyzable.[64] Therefore, Wuthnow might very well be on point when predicting that "both the politics and the epistemology of higher education suggest that the study of religion and personal expressions of faith will remain on the margins."[65]

In sum, because the identity politics discourse demands that religious identities also be validated and accommodated, secular universities and colleges have been put in a position to reengage with religion. They have managed to navigate this reengagement strategically by narrowly construing expressions of faith in terms of religious identity and making accommodations for religious spaces, rituals, and even certain religious practices, without necessarily legitimizing religious beliefs and expressions as epistemologically relevant or as sources of truth.

Postsecularity

This ultimately brings us to the twenty-first century, which scholars note is now characteristic of a "postsecular" world. Jacobsen and Jacobsen argue that we are in a "postsecular America" because religion and religious orientations continue to endure. They use the term "postsecular" to mean that secularization theory does not reflect on-the-ground realities since religion has not disappeared; rather, the new century has brought with it a renewed interest in religion in various forms. In their later work, Jacobsen and Jacobsen note that the postsecular age is illustrative of a "pluriform" era in higher education, where religion is no longer invisible or private and is engaged with in various ways.[66] In such a postsecular academy, scholars argue, religion not only survives but thrives,[67] often providing evidence of accommodation and interfaith encounters as examples of that thriving. Even Marsden, writing in *The Soul of the American University Revisited*, contends that postsecularity is now the commonplace descriptor of our time and of higher education specifically. Engaging with Schmaulzbauer and Mahoney, Patel, and others, he defines postsecularity as the fact that "secularism is not steadily triumphing as religion inevitably recedes in the face of modernity."[68]

The term "postsecularity," of course, subsumes certain meanings about secularity both in terms of its trajectory and its positionality. In other words, for us to be in a postsecular time when religion endures, we would supposedly have gone through a secular time when religion was either disappearing or thought to be disappearing. This would make secularity both linear and contra-religion. As I have discussed above, such a conventional understanding of all things secular is simplistic not only because religion and secularity are not necessarily epistemic opposites (as Asad, Mahmood, Taylor, and others have discussed) but also because secularity itself is largely a Protestant product. How, then, should we understand the term "postsecular"?

This is the very question that Gorski et al. explore in their edited volume, *The Post-Secular in Question.*[69] They present the example of Peter Berger—who initially popularized the secularization thesis and later reversed his position—to ask: "Bearing in mind such shifts in the thought of a major sociologist and social thinker like Berger, we ask: Is it the social scientists' vision that is crooked, while the historical road is straight?"[70] In other words, they question whether there has been an actual shift in the world "out there" vis-à-vis the state of religion (and secularity) or whether that state has always been the same but has just been understood in different (and sometimes incorrect) ways by scholars. They write:

> The question of the post-secular poses two lines of inquiry: first, determinations about the state of religiosity in the world; second, understanding the new ways that social scientists, philosophers, historians, and scholars from across disciplines are and are not paying attention to religion. In other words, the question is: Which world has changed—the "real" one or the scholarly one? To some degree, contributors to this book argue that the answer is "both."[71]

For my project, I ask the same question of the place of religion and secularity in higher education, and thus the efficacy of using the term "postsecular" in this context. Jacobsen and Jacobsen's usage of the term[72] and their contention that religion is "no longer invisible" would imply that religion was, at some point, invisible in higher education or that higher education was secular and is now postsecular. However, drawing on Gorski et al.'s provocation, I argue that the "historical road" of religion and secularity in higher education has been largely "straight" when viewed from the perspective of a non-Protestant religious group such as Muslim students. More specifically, the place of religion and secularity in higher education has always been mediated by Protestant ideas and goals, even if those ideas and goals have undergone varying levels of visibility over time. Even those who lament the "golden age" of Protestant influence in the academy, such as Marsden, do acknowledge that ideals now touted by American higher education especially—such as tolerance, peacemaking, racial and social justice, among others—"all had among their direct antecedents liberal Protestantism"[73] and that it remains difficult to disentangle these influences from decidedly secular ones. For this reason, the "pluriform" era of higher education cannot be understood without considering the Protestant influence on religion and secularity.

I argue, thus, that the BU campus context of Muslim students is neither entirely postsecular nor post-Protestant. Rather, it is more appropriately understood as a *Protestant–secular* context.[74] What do I mean by this term particularly in the campus context?

Protestant Secularity

Before I answer that question, let me reiterate some takeaways from our journey up to this point: the categories of secularity and religion have a Protestant lineage that, historically, was brazenly overt in American culture and institutions, including higher education. In recent times, even though Protestant orientations endure, they have become more elusive and difficult to disentangle from secularity especially. This is because secularity and religion are often treated as binaries and "the secular" is presumed to be religion-neutral. The problem, then, is that while higher education institutions like BU claim secularity, the complexity and nuance of that concept is lost because we assume that these institutions treat religion objectively. Instead, such institutions have had a historical bias toward Protestantism, a stake in producing secularity, and in presenting that secularity to be impartial vis-à-vis religion.

Given this history and such bias, how then should we describe the context of an institution such as BU? In the conversation with which I began this chapter, Zara described BU as "secular by name but actually so religious" or, in more theoretical terms—Protestant–secular. Although the term owes its coinage to Fessenden,[75] it has since been generative in the field of American religion. McCreary and Wheatley[76] offer a good definition:

> Secularization has been an epistemological and social process aligned with the rise of Protestantism, such that Protestantism begets a regime we might call 'secularism' or even an ideology, mood, or episteme called 'the secular.' Among scholars of American religion, this thesis—evident in the formulation 'the Protestant secular'—has become popular in recent years.[77]

In their work, however, McCreary and Wheatley in fact question the continued theoretical efficacy of the concept:

> The popularization of the Protestant secular thesis has been a productive development in the historiography of American religion. We argue, though, that this framework has been stretched beyond its capacity. Without a doubt, modern subjectivities owe a great deal to Protestant ideologies, but in what ways is it illuminative to call individualism and privatism 'Protestant' and/or 'secular'? In some cases, this labeling could be an early step toward a compelling analysis. In others, though, it might emit an air of perspicacity without clarifying much at all.[78]

I mention their critique here to note precisely how it *is*, in fact, illuminative for me to use the "Protestant–secular" as an analytical tool in the context of this study. Even if the concept has been "stretched beyond its capacity" in the field of American religion, it can offer a "compelling analysis" to the study of religion in higher education. This is so for two reasons.

First, barring a few notable interventions, research on religion in higher education generally does not pay sufficient attention to the Protestant influence on religion and secularity or to the fact that such privileged notions of religion do not necessarily map on to the experience of non-Protestants.[79] Through the case of Muslim students at BU, I interrogate those narratives. Therefore, it is useful for me to consider the BU context as a Protestant–secular one, by which I mean that the secularity of the campus is mediated by Protestant features. By extension, then, religious engagement and encounter on campus is also mediated by Protestant features.

Second, and relatedly, applying the "Protestant–secular" to understand the experience of a religio-racial minority population on campus is a departure from frameworks typically applied to the study of minorities in higher education. This is intentional. In understanding the experience of BU Muslim students, I could have applied other conceptual frameworks, such as multiculturalism, identity politics, or identity development, to name a few.[80] However, my contention is that these frameworks presuppose that minorities are minorities, taking that as the point of departure to explore their experiences and offer recommendations. To be sure, I am not claiming in my project that Muslim students are not minorities; however, my point of departure is to interrogate broader historical hegemonies and their institutional legacies that produce and reproduce this minority status. In other words, for us to comprehensively understand the tensions that Muslim students encounter at a secular campus, we must take into consideration the very nature of that secularity—hence my application of the "Protestant–secular" framework.

Additionally, I want to distinguish usage of the "Protestant–secular" term from other terms utilized in recent scholarship on religion and secularity in higher education, such as "Christian privilege." More specifically, the term "Christian privilege" and critical religion scholarship have been critiqued for ignoring "Christian complexity" and "secular privilege" in higher education. Christian communities, it is said, are diverse and, in some cases, also impacted and marginalized by the privilege that secularity wields.[81] Critical religion scholars such as Jenny Small and Sachi Edwards[82] have responded to this critique at great length, illustrating how Christian normativity continues to permeate American society, whether in the form of calendars and holidays,[83] discourse and language,[84] or values and norms.[85] With respect to this debate, I want to be deliberate in my labeling of the BU context as a Protestant-secular one, versus a Christian or a secular one. I do so precisely to note that the relationship between secularity and religion(s) is dominated by a *particular* type of religious orientation rooted in and entangled with mainline liberal Protestantism, as historical trajectories in the United States broadly and in higher education specifically have illustrated. Moreover, as Small et al. note, "In the specific context of American higher education, secularism portrays neutrality while concealing Protestant Christian normativity."[86] In my rendering, this normativity manifests via secularity having Protestant features, which then mediate how minority religious students engage with their religious traditions. Because of this dialectic, I find a "Protestant–secular" label to be more specific and apt than a "Christian-secular," a "Christian privilege," or a "secular privilege" one. In this way, my contention is that the overarching regime is both/and—that is, both Protestant and secular.

I will note here that my Muslim student interlocutors do not necessarily think about secularity in those terms—that is, as having Protestant features. Barring Zara's incisive comment about BU being secular but actually religious, the students did not, at any point, have a conversation with me regarding the historical legacy or deconstruction of secularity. Rather, their responses to and inhabitation of being Muslim at a secular campus revealed their expectation of secularity as epistemically contra-religion without a bias toward any one particular religion. They took BU's secularity as such as a given, just as they took their minority status within this context also as a given. They consistently framed their Muslim experiences within discourses of identity politics and campus diversity, but they did not mention the entanglement of secularity and liberal pluralism with Protestantism.[87] For this reason, too,

I find it illuminating to apply the "Protestant–secular" framing to understand their experiences because the students' silence and obliviousness to it affirm its power on campus.

In using that concept, however, I am in no way suggesting that Islam or Muslim students at BU *become* Protestant or even adopt wholesale Protestant features. Instead, my project is an investigation of how Muslim students, given their *Muslim* orientation—as opposed to a Protestant orientation—experience Muslim life and Islam at a secular campus, given that secularity (as a knowledge regime) and religion (as a category) have Protestant underpinnings. The ultimate consideration is always how Muslim students negotiate Islam and being Muslim on campus in a secular setting, but with attention to the complexity and nuance of that secularity as *not* religion-neutral.

2

Pluralism's Power: Muslim Inclusion on Protestant Terms

One evening, Amira and Amani, two sophomores I was shadowing, were attending a concert on campus. This wasn't a typical concert, however. It was a "Mawlid" concert—an event to celebrate the birthday of the Prophet Muhammad—held at Bellington University (BU) for the first time in its 100+ years history. Zaynab, the BU Muslim chaplain, introduced the event by emphasizing the significance of the Prophet Muhammad for Muslims particularly and for the world generally. She noted his commitment to inclusion and diversity and how fitting it was that his life was being celebrated at the BU's church, which itself was a "symbol of inclusion."

The program featured several student performances, including a Quranic recitation by Amani, but the highlight of the event was a Sufi ensemble visiting from Spain. At one point, the group performed "Salawat"—a traditional Muslim song in praise of the Prophet Muhammad. The song has been rendered in different tunes, languages, and styles across history and cultures. This one was being performed in Arabic with Celtic music, given the group's multicultural background. Seated at the chancel in the brightly lit auditorium under images of Christian saints, Jesus and his disciples, the Nativity, the Crucifixion, and the Ascension, the vocalists sang, "O God, send peace and blessings upon Muhammad" while the instrumentalists played a harmonizing melody. Admittedly, this was one of the more popular performances to which the audience sang along. The event, free and open to the public, had been publicized heavily, and the church's pews were quite full.

Being Muslim on Campus. Abiya Ahmed, Oxford University Press. © Oxford University Press 2026.
DOI: 10.1093/9780197773628.003.0003

One of the many campus visitors that evening might easily have concluded that irrespective of whether BU was a religiously affiliated or secular campus, it institutionally supported religious pluralism. After all, a grand celebration of Islam's central figure at the university's historic church would seem to indicate the triumph of religious diversity and inclusion.

Not too long after, I found Amira and asked her about the event. "How was it? Did you enjoy that?"

"The music was good, but in all honesty I'm not really into classical music so I got really bored at some points. And I was wondering what my relatives would be thinking if they were at this scene," she replied.

"What would they think?"

"I mean, they're very traditional and they would think this is wrong in all sorts of ways, you know." She looked at me, expecting me to know, but I probed, "Wrong how?"

She laughed and then remarked, "Oh it was interesting. I was looking around in there and I was like, paintings of Jesus and of saints and stuff . . . I was just like wow; it's come to this." Amira thought the interfaith nature of the Mawlid celebration was strange. She wasn't particularly "moved" by the event, and she admitted that she didn't really leave the event feeling any more religious or "any closer to the Prophet," which, according to her, would be the purpose of celebrating his life. She also thought that not only her relatives back in Malaysia but also her local community would find BU's event an unfamiliar mode of celebrating the Mawlid.

Her reactions are telling, especially because in an earlier conversation, Zara had made similar comments to me: "I don't think people are doing this to honor the Prophet or celebrate his birth, they don't even know when he was born. But I think that to gain whatever sense of religion, they feel that they need this . . . that it's good for them." Zara also thought the event, with all its interfaith glory, was "trademark Bellington University. It fits right into what they believe in, what they're trying to promote."

"Which is . . . ?" I asked.

"Which is, this more inclusive view of what religion is, and bringing people together through music and events and ritual," she replied, without skipping a beat.

Ostensibly, there is nothing irregular about music, events, and ritual as a means of gathering a diverse set of people. In fact, BU's Mawlid epitomizes the very kind of "interfaith encounter" that experts like Diana Eck and Eboo Patel would commend as promoting religious pluralism. As Eck[1] has noted, diversity is a fact, whereas "pluralism is a response to diversity, an engagement with diversity."[2] Patel, founder of the Interfaith Youth Core (IFYC), now rebranded as Interfaith America, has drawn on Eck's work to define "religious pluralism as active engagement of religious diversity to a constructive end."[3] BU's Mawlid is just one example of how the university, at the institutional level, attempts to engage religious diversity by publicly commemorating an Islamic occasion that is important to Muslims. We might reasonably expect Muslim students to be enthusiastic about such engagement.

They were not. As Zara's and Amira's comments indicate, they were mostly apathic or critical. In this chapter, I delve deeper into why that is so. As an institution, BU engages Muslim students in various ways, including marking Islamic celebrations such as Ramadan, Eid, and the Mawlid. This is meant to illustrate its commitment to fostering inclusion and diversity on campus. But how Muslim students view and engage with these accommodations and celebrations is also illustrative of how BU perpetuates what Bender and Klassen call "prescriptive pluralism": the sort of pluralism that "recognizes some kinds of religious interactions and encounters and some kinds of religions (but not others) as normal and natural."[4] Contributors to their edited volume *After Pluralism* explore how pluralism works at sites such as theater, prisons, and interfaith coalitions, to name a few. Following their lead, in this chapter I explore dimensions of religious pluralism at a secular campus and how Muslim students interact with it. Patel has described college campuses as "mini civil societies" that are fertile ground for the work of pluralism.[5] Exploring how BU engages in pluralism sheds light on how Muslim students experience "prescriptive pluralism" at their campus and how that is a Protestant–secular feature that exercises power over and mediates these students' lived experience.

At BU, the workings of pluralism and Muslim students' engagement with it reveals a complex picture of campus religious pluralism—one that privileges Protestant conceptions of religion even at a secular—and therefore purportedly neutral vis-à-vis religion—institution. Pluralism's historical trajectory and relationship with American civics help us make sense of this picture. Thus, I begin with situating pluralism historically and within the discourse of civic ideals, as articulated by some of its strongest proponents. Following this lineage, I discuss pluralism in the BU context, illustrating Muslim student perspectives on how their campus accommodates or engages them. I conclude with a discussion of the pluralism discourse today, maintaining that, at minimum, an acknowledgment of power and privilege must be central to how we frame and understand diversity and difference.

Pluralism on Protestant Terms

In *The Protestant Voice in American Pluralism*, Martin Marty chronicles the relationship between Protestantism and pluralism.[6] He points out that from the seventeenth century until about the mid-twentieth century, Protestants "ran the show" in America, but that changed in the 1950s with the emergence of various religious groups and options both within and outside of Protestantism. Marty contends in his final chapter that most Protestants had no choice but to accept pluralism as a reality of American society. "Still," he writes, "the acceptance has been more hearty and less grudging than we might have expected when compared with how peoples have interacted in other places and other times."[7] Even though Protestantism and Protestant leaders dominated American public culture until the 1950s, he states, America's religious diversity tempered that hegemony by giving voice and weight to marginalized religious groups.

Porterfield makes a similar observation when discussing the end of missionary evangelicalism.[8] Per her account, even as the Protestant influence on pluralism and activism has become "subdued," these impulses in American culture and publics owe their formation to Protestantism, whose hegemonic decline ultimately "created a vacuum in the leadership of American social outreach that many different religious and secular groups stepped in to fill."[9] Porterfield views American religious diversity as an inevitable outcome of the nation's founding as a Protestant country that promoted nondenominational cooperation for the purpose of worldly good. Ultimately, she concludes, "the vitality and pluralism of American social outreach is rooted in American Protestant evangelical and missionary history and, to some extent at least, represents the fruition of that history."[10] In other words, according to Porterfield, the trajectory of Protestantism in America (including its supposed retreat) gives way to religious diversity but always on Protestant terms.

Marty's Protestant "acceptance" and Porterfield's Protestant "subduing" situate Protestantism in America as both the cause and the catalyst for pluralism. Or, if we use Robert P. Jones's analogy of "America gathered around a dining-room table,"[11] it would appear from Marty's and Porterfield's accounts that Protestant Christians, originally the self-proclaimed owners of the table and seated at its head, invited others to join the table and then gave up the "patriarch's position" out of a sense of pragmatism. In reality, as Jones notes, "The chief impediment for pluralism today is not that we have run out of chairs. Rather, it is that many white Christians have been reluctant to relinquish the privileged seat of power."[12] When we explore how Muslim students experience pluralism at a secular campus whose center is an ecumenical church, we see that this is an important historical point to remember because it reminds us of who has power (white Protestant Christianity) and who is the subject of that power (Muslims).

Notably, 1955—which, for Marty, is the year marking the end of Protestants running the show—also marks the publication of Will Herberg's *Protestant-Catholic-Jew*.[13] Herberg's classic work calls attention to the change in the American "religious situation" by asserting that the United States was now a "three religion country" where Protestantism, Catholicism, and Judaism were "equally legitimate" and "equally American."[14] Herberg was fascinated by the fact that a newcomer to America was expected to assimilate in terms of nationality, language, and culture, but not religion, because American religious freedom allowed for the retaining of one's religion. He also contended that America's "common religion" was the "American Way of Life"—a free market economy, egalitarianism and individualism, idealism and morality—all of which was part of American civil life and a strong unifying force. A decade or so later, Robert Bellah[15] would expand on this contention in terms of "Civil Religion in America" by highlighting the religious or sacred nature of language, symbols, rituals, and themes in the American political sphere. Bellah argued that American civil religion, though derived from Christianity and built on Biblical archetypes, was a religion in and of itself. It wasn't quite Protestant Christianity, but the sanctity and celebration of American nationalism, symbols, and ritualscould be seen as a secularized promotion of Protestant themes such as exceptionalism (or being chosen), individual responsibility, and nondenominational cooperation for "redeeming the world."[16] Inevitably, some commentators, such as Marsden, who lament the secularization or "hiding" of Protestantism in this way, argue that this form of pluralism in fact served as a deterrent to a more overt religious Protestant presence, especially in higher education.[17]

But there is also the opposite issue: this form of pluralism nevertheless privileges Protestant themes and values and obfuscates the fact that it does, thus wielding power in ways that are often unclear or confusing. In fact, if we compare Herberg's and Bellah's works, we see how their articulations of the American religious situation and civil religion illustrate the limitations of American religious pluralism.[18] Herberg's "Protestant–Catholic–Jew," while noteworthy for presenting a new status quo, also, in many ways, offers insight into persistence of the status quo. Placing Catholics and Jews alongside Protestants on an equal footing was ambitiously inclusive on Herberg's part. At the same time, however, it was an exclusive move: as Herberg writes, identifying as "a Buddhist, a Muslim, or anything but a Protestant, Catholic, or Jew, even when one's Americanness is otherwise beyond question" is to be "foreign."[19] Herberg wrote before the 1965 Immigration Act that led to an increase in the number of communities of other faiths. Today, experts such as Patel can point to the fact of America's religious diversity to contend that "Protestant–Catholic–Jew" can now be expanded to include people of other religions (or none).[20] However, missing from the conversation is the persistent, hidden, and unquestioned role of Protestant hegemony over pluralism. Even when pluralism claims to include others beyond Herberg's original tri-faith communities, those others "must accept a hegemonic conception of civil religion entangled in the mission of white, Protestant nation builders" and therefore "demonstrate their Americanness and practice their religions in ways that do not disturb others."[21] For Muslim students on campuses such as BU, this is somewhat the case—they often end up practicing their religion in ways that do not disturb others. Sometimes, they internalize their minoritized status, expressing appreciation and contentment for the accommodations they are offered. At the same time, they are also astute in recognizing inclusion for the institution's sake (as in the case of the Mawlid) and are therefore uneasy with the sort of pluralism prescribed by grand events heightening and celebrating their difference.

Pluralism in Civic Terms

Diana Eck and Eboo Patel—two key figures in the story of religion on campus—often construe the value of religious pluralism in civic terms. They also make arguments for pluralism in theological terms, but a central perspective they share is that religious pluralism is an American ideal bounded with civic ideals. As Eck writes, America's founding fathers "were guided by deep religious sensibilities to argue for a civic space that is not shaped by religion" with the ensuing goal of religious freedom for all traditions.[22] Eck is not oblivious to Protestant domination in America. She notes that historically Protestant Christians supported religious freedom but also shaped America in terms of a Christian ethos, even if there was no official established religion. In line with Marty,[23] however, she too thinks that the fact of religious diversity has challenged this ethos and the present-day "civic space" of America as secular in terms of equally valuing all religious traditions.

According to Eck, traditionally there have been two responses to diversity—exclusion and assimilation—both of which are problematic because exclusion leads to marginalization and oppression whereas assimilation leads to conformism. For her, a third and correct response is, of course, pluralism, which has four features: engagement with diversity, active seeking of understanding, encounter of commitments, and dialogue.[24] While Eck is therefore not proposing the "melting pot" approach to diversity, she does believe that the secular civic context renders irrelevant one's religious stances or beliefs, essentially offering everyone a level playing field.

Patel adopts a similar approach, noting that pluralism—religious or otherwise—is a necessary feature of American democracy. In *Out of Many Faiths*, Patel explores the question of religious diversity as it relates to civil religion. His test case is Muslims and Islam in America, and he argues, optimistically, that civil religion is the vehicle through which religious pluralism flourishes in America.[25]

He takes issue with Philip Gorski's contention that civil religion is a Judeo-Christian formation, noting that "its genius" is that it "expands the national narrative in a manner that dignifies previously marginalized occupants."[26] For Patel, Muslims in America acquire space and legitimacy for themselves and for Islam through the mechanism of civil religion and shared (not to mention sacred) national myths.

Both Eck and Patel are optimistic about the practicality of such goals and do not sufficiently consider the dichotomy of theory and practice. Perhaps the best example of this dichotomy is Denise Spellberg's detailed discourse on the question "Could a Muslim be President?" in which she explores an eighteenth-century constitutional debate between Federalists and Anti-Federalists about religious tests for holding office.[27] The debate revolves around the possibility of hypothetical Muslims becoming president.[28] The answer to her question on whether a Muslim could hold the highest office in the land: "Theoretically, yes, but realistically, no."[29] Realistically no, because even though the Muslim presence in America is very much a twenty-first century reality, certain religions continue to "define loyalty" to the state, despite the fact that a religious test is unconstitutional. Spellberg's study is worth reading in its entirety, and her conclusion signals the limits of American ideals with respect to pluralism. In terms of the "dinner table" model, pluralism is wonderful as long as those in power do not have to give up their seat.

Another relevant example is the controversy surrounding the Park 51 (Cordoba House) project in Manhattan, which, while perfectly legal, was not built because of its proximity to Ground Zero. Patel presents the story to trigger critical questions about "Muslim integration into the American experiment"—for him, the Cordoba project was "a Muslim community living out the definition of pluralism and doing so in a way that was symbolic enough to be registered in American civil religion."[30] Evidently, however, Muslims "living out pluralism" in *this* particular way would not work. Discussing the same controversy, Rosemary Hicks explains why: "secularism in the United States has never been neutral or antireligious but accommodates particular kinds of Protestant practices more than, and sometimes to the exclusion of Catholic, Jewish, Muslim, and other traditions (such as Native Americans') that were not originally considered "religious" or relevant to First Amendment protections."[31] In other words, as she writes, constructing a Muslim community center close to Ground Zero would allow Muslims a level of religious freedom that, although legal and protected, was still considered inappropriate by political officials and lobbyists. Ultimately, building on Bender and Klassen,[32] Hicks concludes that "pluralism is a mode of controlling for difference, based on *particular* interpretations of religion that are assumed to be *universally* shared."[33] We might reasonably wonder whether any controversy would have been generated if the project in question was a Protestant Christian one. Thus, while both Eck and Patel acknowledge that pluralism is a process and a work in progress, neither sufficiently considers the power and privileges, and therefore the boundaries and contradictions, embedded in the history and practice of pluralism.

In contrast, William Hutchison offers a more textured history of religious pluralism as a contentious ideal, showing how it was not something that was always easily accepted as a motif of national unity.[34] Moreover, he also discusses how religious pluralism was and continues to be—as we see today—tied to racial logics and liberal or conservative political alignments. Compared to Eck and Patel, he presents the relationship between pluralism and democracy as more fraught. We see this nuance also in John Inazu's counter to Patel: Inazu writes that not only are we not as united as Patel imagines, but also our current legal protections are not sufficient for us to be united while retaining our differences. As he notes, "for much of our country's history, white Protestants established a cultural and legal baseline into which other religious believers had to assimilate."[35] Thus, apart from the fact that white Protestant Christians are not as willing to give up the seat of power, there is also the issue of enduring Protestant influence. Even if we concede that Protestantism is no longer at the head of Jones's metaphorical dining table and is perhaps now seated alongside other religions or belief systems, can we really expect that centuries worth of influence and power while it *was* in that seat will have suddenly vanished or shifted? Inazu thinks not, though he makes a special plea to white Protestants[36] to recommit to religious pluralism "at a time in which they retain a significant amount of privilege even as aspects of their privilege are being weakened."[37]

Notwithstanding the question of whether pluralism is the ethos which warrants wholehearted commitment in today's climate, there is also the question of whether such a commitment is even possible. For example, Bellah himself was less optimistic about such Protestant commitment. Here he is again, four decades after "Civil Religion," still articulating—though perhaps more explicitly—the Protestant structure of American culture:

> Since I am arguing that American culture is Protestant to the bone and has affected very cultural and religious group more than they realize, I am putting a special burden on all non-Protestant groups, particularly the largest one, namely Catholics, to nurture a genuine multiculturalism in a very hostile environment.[38]

Bellah is confident that religion is crucial to pluralism in America (the "only sustainable basis" for it, as he describes), but he is also aware of the Protestant stronghold on American culture. In economic terms, Protestantism will always have what Peter Berger calls a "comparative advantage" over other religious traditions because participation in pluralism is underwritten by Protestant features.[39] Given such an advantage, it will remain challenging for non-Protestant traditions to be equal partners in the pluralism project.

In outlining the above perspectives on religious pluralism especially in civic terms, I want to emphasize two main points: first, the Protestant voice in American religious pluralism continues to have power not only because it has been the sole voice for so long, but also because it is still the loudest. Second, construing religious pluralism as a feature of civic ideals might not be as contentious in theory, but it is in practice. This is because for groups like Muslims, their participation in pluralism is contingent on their religious practice and beliefs being *just different enough* to be "included," while also aligning with (or, at the very least, not vocally contradicting) Protestant ideas of religious practice and beliefs. In other words, Muslims must make their Islam and Muslimness *legible* to be included as civic participants. Whenever they depart from such legibility and threaten the status quo, they are likely to be excluded or to exclude themselves from the pluralism project.

Pluralism at BU

Such tensions reproduce on campus. My encounters with students and my observations of events at BU illustrate that in a secular institution of higher education where religious diversity is seriously engaged with and pluralism is a core value, Protestant Christianity does, indeed, continue to have an advantage. How do Muslim students experience this advantage? That is the question to which I turn next.

As noted above, Patel considers college campuses as "mini civil societies" that are fertile ground for the work of pluralism.[40] He is not alone in this consideration, as higher education has seen a surge in diversity initiatives in the last decade or so, even as many of those efforts are now under threat due to new federal guidelines.[41] Even when inclusion efforts were made, however, the primary focus was racial/ethnic, gender, and class diversity,[42] and despite many colleges being more diverse, inequality has persisted.[43] Still, religious diversity has received *some* attention, especially following research on and advocacy for students' spiritual and religious lives on campus.[44] Jacobsen and Jacobsen refer to this time period as the "pluriform" era of religion and higher education, where religion is valuable and seriously engaged.[45]

In addition, the work of research initiatives such as Eck's The Pluralism Project and organizations such as Patel's Interfaith America have brought into sharper focus religious diversity and pluralism in higher education. According to Patel, his organization aims to curate

> high-quality, sustainable interfaith programming at every level of a college campus, from the strategic plan to the content of first-year student orientations.... At DePaul University in Chicago, for example, different religious groups have their own worship space (demonstrating respect for identity), the University Ministry staff runs interfaith dialogue programs (building relationships across religious communities), and the Center for Service Learning proactively engages them in interfaith service efforts that improve Chicago (contributing to the common good). This is an excellent illustration of [how] colleges can create arrangements that engage diversity positively and proactively.[46]

We can easily replace "DePaul University" with "Bellington University" in Patel's example because it, too, engages religious diversity in this manner. Patel's perspective is that of the curator, but how do students view and engage with such institutional efforts? Studies on the correlation between campus climate and students' pluralism competence or orientation show that institutional context plays a role in students' worldviews and attitudes,[47] but much of this research is quantitative. As Small and Bowman have noted, "This is the time to move away from generalizations and into more concrete specifics . . . the kind of descriptive information yielded by qualitative studies (conversations with students and faculty, along with institutional case studies) will also be necessary for investigating these topics further."[48]

In this vein, I present a glimpse of Muslim life at BU through the students' perspectives of their institution, categorized as follows: religious accommodations; religious discourse, and religious encounter (via the case of the Mawlid). Each of these can be considered a dimension of pluralism and offers a critique of it by explicating its limitations for Muslim students.

Religious Accommodation: "They're Great about That!"

A good place to begin is religious space. Applying a geographic perspective to religious pluralism in America, Bret E. Carroll argues that spatial politics are critical to this discourse.[49] As he illustrates, religious spaces can be sites of contestation when conflicts occur (such as the Park51 mosque controversy or vandalism of religious places); or sites of collaboration when interfaith cooperation occurs, such as the sharing of space by a Methodist Church and a mosque in Fremont, California—an example that Eck also uses often.[50] Like Patel, Carroll correlates worship space with the development and respect of religious identity, and he is accurate in noting the role of sacred space in religious pluralism. For example, Wendy Cadge has shown how hospital chapels in America are moving from a primary Protestant Christian orientation to a more diverse one.[51] Similarly, Sophie Gilliat-Ray's work on sacred spaces in British public institutions such as prisons, hospitals, and universities also indicates this shift.[52]

At BU, a secular campus, there is no shortage of religious and/or spiritual spaces. The Religious Life Office (RLO) oversees multiple such spaces, the primary one being the university's church, a central feature of the campus. There is also a contemplative space on campus, which is not identifably religious. Finally, RLO oversees the curation and operation of several prayer rooms for different faiths and a few meeting spaces at the student center. Chaplains from various religions—including Jewish and Muslim—also have their offices here. If the BU Church is a commanding Protestant presence on campus, the student center, though nowhere as outstanding as the church, certainly offers a more neutral orientation. In addition to the Muslim prayer room, the student center contains a separate larger room, where the Muslim Friday congregational prayer is held. This is meant to be a multifaith space, with large windows, comfortable cushions, rows of chairs, and artwork representing various religious traditions, including Christianity, Judaism, Islam, Hinduism, and Buddhism. On a given day, it can be used as is, or it can be converted into a space for different religious learning activities or rituals. There are also *wudu* (ablution) stations for Muslim students to wash up before prayer.

In addition to having designated space, there are other features of Muslim life at BU. The Muslim Student Association (MSA) works with RLO to provide dawn and fast-breaking meals every day in Ramadan for those observing the month. Each year, a few of the university's highest officials attend an *iftar* (fast-breaking meal), and the president's office sometimes sends out an official letter to the MSA at the start of Ramadan honoring the month and its significance. The end of Ramadan is marked by a public Eid celebration held on campus, open to all. Another important feature of Muslim life at BU is *halal* meal options at all the dining halls and selected *halal* options at several on-campus eateries.

With this in mind, Muslim students were largely appreciative of these features at BU. As Yusuf, a sophomore and MSA board member, told me, "Praying, fasting, those sorts of things, I haven't ever been publicly discriminated against, and BU has made it so much easier for us." This sentiment was common, and several students pointed out to me that they have been able to perform their daily prayers on campus not just in the designated prayer room but also sometimes at the Mosaic Cultural Center (MCC) or in empty hallways, stairways, and classrooms. The ritual of *Salah*—the Islamic prayer—can be completed easily and quickly almost anywhere, though its performance in public continues to hold social and political ramifications in the American imagination.[53] During my observations at BU, I spent many of my breaks in the Muslim prayer room, and students would be in and out. I also did observe a student praying outdoors on the grass once, though this was not a common occurrence.

For BU Muslim students, having designated prayer space on campus, holding Friday congregational prayers, celebrating Eid and Ramadan, having *halal* food options on campus—these are all indicators of successful efforts at claiming space on campus. Much of the research on pluralism on campus specific to Muslim students includes analyses and recommendations of these very factors.[54] Khalil, an African American sophomore, especially appreciated the Ramadan iftar meals and the *suhoor* boxes (dawn meals), and Amira summarized the general student sentiment as follows: "I haven't had any accommodation issues as a Muslim on campus. They're great about that!"

At the same time, it is important to remember Protestantism's comparative advantage and the related history out of which a pluralist perspective emerges. As far as spatial dynamics go, Gilliat-Ray is correct in highlighting how "the fact that Muslims in some instances have *achieved* their own exclusive space, but have also had spaces *provided* for their sole use, is a poignant reminder of the fact that sacred space is almost inevitably 'entangled in politics.'"[55] Such an entanglement is also indicative of power dynamics, which, in this case, have to do with Protestant Christianity being the dominant worldview even at a secular campus. As Mayhew, Bowman, and Rockenbach explain, religious minority and nonreligious students hold positive views on their campus climate likely because "the dominant religious narrative may be codified in many similar institutional practices (e.g., scheduling winter break around Christmas; see Seifert 2007) but not reinforced (e.g., celebrating only Christmas on campus)."[56] Relatedly, Bryant has shown how religious minorities tend to have higher levels of an ecumenical worldview than majority students.[57]

Given the lopsided power relations, this should not surprise us. All the students I spent time with and interviewed repeatedly expressed appreciation for BU's "accommodations" of their Muslim needs. Even Zara, often the sharpest critic of campus religious-secular dynamics, noted that "BU has been very accommodating of our needs as Muslims." One way to analyze such appreciation is to take Patel's approach and consider this pluralistic progress.[58] Hadia Mubarak, the first female president of the MSA National, observed over a decade ago, "Of all religious requirements, the ability to fulfill Islam's religious mandate to pray five times a day is of primary concern to Muslim students. Securing a clean and relatively quiet space to pray their daily prayers on campus is perhaps the most important religious accommodation that Muslim students seek in college."[59] Placed in historical context of Muslim student needs and advocacy such accommodations at BU are definitely progress.

But we should not stop there because we can also understand Muslim students' appreciation of their university's "accommodation" of what might be considered basic needs in another way. Taking from Bellah and his assertion of how American society's Protestant structure has affected other groups more than they might realize, we can understand these students' perspectives in terms of having—to some extent at least—internalized Protestant Christian privilege in the guise of secularity. In discussing "accommodations" that BU made for Muslims, even their usage of the term "accommodation" is indicative of such internalization. Moreover, none of the students mentioned, for example, that the weekly holiday was Sunday or that winter break was organized around Christmas, markers of normalized Christian privilege.[60]

In stark contrast to the Stanford graduate student I mentioned in the Preface, who took issue with her training scheduled around Ramadan and Eid, these BU undergraduates instead very much appreciate professors and administrators who accommodated their needs. Here is Zara again on this issue, "If you go up to the professor and you're like, 'Hi, I'm fasting, I need this to be an hour earlier, an hour later or like the next day,' they will probably understand. But beyond that, how much else can you expect them to do? They're not going to change the class schedule just for us." On one of the days that I followed Yusuf around campus and through his classes, he appeared to seamlessly integrate his daily schedule and prayer obligations. But after his late morning Japanese class (he was planning a semester abroad in Japan), he told me, "You picked a good day to follow me; it's so busy though and I usually skip my next CS lecture." How come, I asked? "Well, it has an odd timing in that it conflicts with lunch and the noon prayer. I usually go pray *dhuhr* (noon prayer) after this (Japanese class) and then have lunch." As we walked to the Muslim prayer room, he elaborated, as if to justify missing his class, "It's just android programming and like learning a skill, so attendance is not really mandatory as long as you do the weekly tasks. You can learn it on YouTube."

Yusuf's own accommodation of his prayer times and Zara's matter-of-fact observation on reasonable expectations from faculty indicate that the power dynamics have been so heavily unequal that religious diversity can complicate matters of pluralism but not necessarily equalize them, as Gilliat-Ray notes:

> Minority faith traditions are struggling to achieve participation, recognition, or 'equality' (sometimes very successfully), but these efforts take place within a framework created by a history and tradition of which they were not a part. Thus, questions remain as to just how 'equal' they can be.[61]

The perceived secularity of Christian symbols, buildings, and holidays makes equality even more difficult to achieve and inequality even more difficult to recognize. BU Muslim students, however, are not completely blind to religious privilege and inequality. Elements of such recognition are manifest in their uneasiness and perplexity surrounding the Mawlid event, which I discuss later in this chapter. Next, however, I present their perspectives on religion in campus discourse, which brings into sharper focus issues of privilege and inequality.

Religious Discourse: "Swept under the rug"

Another dimension of an ideal pluralism is to invite and include diverse kinds of religious discourse and dialogue.[62] As Patel has written, "in American civil religion we do not deify a position so much as we sacralize a discourse, including the inevitable tensions, as long as said discourse follows certain norms and observes basic parameters."[63] The ensuing question, of course, is who decides these norms and parameters? When is religious discourse acceptable on campus, and what kind of discourse?

Notably, when I asked Muslim students about Muslim life on campus, their immediate responses were almost exclusively about campus accommodations of their religious *practice*: prayer space, dietary needs, and holiday celebrations. On those matters, as I have shown above, there was consensus that BU was faring well. On religious discourse, however, the picture becomes considerably more complex. I asked students to tell me about their general observations of the role of religion in campus discourse; as well as about their own personal experience of discussing religion on campus, whether in class or in interpersonal conversations. Such probing prompted more contemplation on their part: the same students who were appreciative of BU's accommodations of practice were less confident about the role of religion in campus discourse. In their responses we see an awareness of when, where, and how it was possible to engage in religious discourse.

Yusuf explained the issue by differentiating between practice and discourse: "I've struggled sometimes but only internally, like not in terms of practicing at BU but on having conversations about or around religion. Religion doesn't necessarily come up in deeper conversations about politics, race, society, things like that." Amira had a similar reaction: "BU definitely is a place where religion feels like it's swept under the rug. Religion is expected to be on the back burner in your daily interactions with a lot of other people on campus. I find myself in places where I don't mention religion, I self-censor, especially when I'm talking about political issues." Idris offered a similar response, including specifics: "It's a bad idea to make a religious argument for LGBTQ or abortion or whatever, because most of the time you're talking to people who are secular." None of these students felt it was possible or even necessary to bring in religion or religious perspectives on issues that were perhaps, to them, not explicitly about religion (race, politics, society, for example) but obviously implicitly connected in their minds for them to mention them. Khalil was the only one who said he had had "occasional" conversations with people about his understanding of religion and found them to be respectful; he also added, however, that "when it comes to my religion, I tend to let it inform me rather than enact an effort to project it. I would much rather let my actions speak for themselves in terms of who I am as opposed to wearing it on my sleeve in order to stand out."

Apprehensions around "standing out" were evident throughout my conversations with Muslim students, and they self-censored accordingly not just in the context of contentious political issues (as Amira had mentioned), but otherwise too. "Talking about religion makes you unseemly, it really does," Ayesha told me once. "I remember there's this café night we were going to do, that dorms do every quarter, and it's basically a talent show. Like a cultural talent show. And I wanted to sing with my friend Hajar. I wanted to sing "*tala'al badru 'alayna,*" and I was like we can talk a little bit about it and explain the history.[64] And we'll call it an Islamic song that we used to sing from childhood. And Hajar was like, 'I think we should just call it an Arabic song.' She was saying, I think, that even though people say that we support Muslims and all that, they don't *really* support Muslims. That's what she was saying. And I was like, 'I guess?' And so, we ended up not singing the song."

"You ended up not singing the song?" I clarified. "No," Ayesha replied. "Did you end up singing anything?" I asked. Ayesha sighed, "No. I was like 'Never mind.' "

Ayesha's and Hajar's remarks are indicative of a Du Boisian "double-consciousness" in that they are acutely aware of potential problematic perceptions that others might impose upon them, should they sing an Islamic song. They are also indicative of their own awareness of the limits of pluralism—"Even though people say we support Muslims and all that, they don't *really* support Muslims." Therefore, even in an institution that claims both secularity and pluralism, Ayesha's comment and experience reveal the boundaries of both. These boundaries are not formal articulations or explicit university policy; however, the institutional context informally signals to these students what they are.

Such awareness, double-consciousness, and self-censorship of religious discourse become even more evident when we look at the students who observe the *hijab*. Asked about these issues, Zara noted, "Look, I think BU is more religious of a place than it thinks it is, and religion is pretty central to the students' lives. But, in conversation everyone thinks *everyone else* at BU is not religious, because you're not supposed to be, right? So, it doesn't come up." She explained that she herself consciously avoids bringing up religious perspectives on political or controversial issues to prevent affirming stereotypes others may have about her: "I'm already at a disadvantage when people see me," she noted, pointing to her *hijab*. "They already expect me to be a certain kind of person, like a backward *hijabi*. And if the first thing I do is talk about religion and religious politics, I'm gone. So, I don't want to play into that, and I stay out of conversations about religion."

Zara's comments indicate how practice and discourse overlap for the students on campus, even if they are not explicitly aware of it. As Williams and Vashi have shown in their study of college-age

Muslim women, the *hijab* continues to be a source of negotiation of religious and social identities.[65] For Zara, its visibility impacts her choices about discourse. She was actually quite certain that the BU context is more religious than it appears, but she was also aware that the secular ethos demands that religion remain private, which is why "everyone thinks everyone else at BU is not religious." In her case, her *hijab* complicates matters as it betrays her Muslim identity. Because of that, she believed that others will already have preconceived notions about her religiosity and that bringing religion into discourse will only reinforce those notions. To mitigate that effect, she made a conscious effort to avoid religious discourse. Relatedly, Amani, who also wore the *hijab*, told me that she sometimes intentionally wears it in the form of a turban. "I feel like I don't want people to project more into it than necessary." What would happen if she consistently wore it in what she considered a more traditional fashion? "People would probably create superficial contextualization," she replied. "I don't want people's minds to go there. Let's keep ambiguity about who or what kind of Muslim I am so I can have conversations on a more objective level." Amani's intentional choices about her *hijab* styles illustrate how BU Muslim students modify their religious practice to make it more palatable to their peers and professors in order to have more credibility in discourse.

We can understand their choices by considering "the paradox of religious pluralism," as Robert Nash explains: "before pluralistic dialogue can begin in earnest, on a college campus it must become 'unbounded.'"[66] Commenting on Stephen Carter's "bounded discourse"—"an arena in which some ideas can be debated and others cannot"—Nash argues that it facilitates systematic exclusion of religious ideas across campus and in dialogue: "Our benevolent, liberal understanding that students' religious and spiritual inclinations are best left to the private sphere of life automatically rules out of bounds any public conversation about these issues that makes us feel uncomfortable."[67] In order for religious pluralism to thrive on campus, says Nash, religion and religious ideas must be allowed entry in realms beyond religious studies departments, student religious associations, or campus ministries. Ayesha and Hajar's cultural talent show would be one such realm.

However, the Protestant–secular idea that religion should stay relegated to the private sphere guides how and when Muslim students engage in religious discourse. Their own notions of what is acceptable is further cemented by their double-consciousness in a world where Islamophobia and anti-Muslim racism persist on college campuses.[68] This further mutes their ability to configure religion and/or spirituality in their discourses. The silence of alternative religious and spiritual epistemologies and perspectives preserves what appears to be a neutral status quo, but is, in fact, the unconstrainted persistence of Protestant Christianity, given its privilege and power.[69] Ultimately, this hinders *true* pluralism. At BU, the way Muslim students view the place and perception of their own religious discourse is a direct critique of the institution's prescriptive pluralism. To them, such a pluralism appears to be saying, "You're welcome to be Muslim but keep your Islam private"—and so to the extent that they can (barring visible sartorial markers), they do.

But in order for such a pluralism to be successful, there must be *some* recognizable difference. Moreover, that difference must be magnified by the institution so that it can be subsequently celebrated and presented as part of the larger pluralism project. I turn next to an instance of that celebration.

Religious Encounter—Mawlid at a Church: "Wow, it's come to this"

Every Friday after the congregational prayer, students would sometimes gather for a lunch sometimes sponsored by the MSA or the RLO. One such Friday, I spotted Zara after the congregational prayer. She waved at me and walked over, asking if I was joining them for lunch. I hesitated because I had to be somewhere else soon, but she quickly said, "It's not pizza! It's going to be some other kind of great food!" We both laughed, and I told her I could stay for a bit.

We walked into the common room, where the buffet lines had already formed. It was evident that there were more males than females present, self-segregated by gender. Not too long after, while Zara and I were chatting over Turkish food about her sociology classes, we heard someone clapping and then, "Can I have everyone's attention please?" It was Zaynab, the RLO Muslim chaplain. She was standing up on a chair to elevate herself so that everyone could see her. As the room quieted down, she announced: "I hope you're all enjoying the food, and I wanted to take your attention from it for just a minute to announce a very important event coming up—the Mawlid concert. RLO is hosting this event, and we are very excited about it for two reasons—first, because for the first time in BU's history, we are going to be celebrating the birthday of the Prophet Muhammad, peace be upon him, on campus. And second, and, even more exciting is that it's being held at the university's church. As you all know, the church is a space for everyone, and it can hold up to 1,200 people, so the more the merrier if you want to bring family and friends!" She was about to step down, and then she joked, "Who thinks the Mawlid is *bid'ah* [innovation]?"[70] She laughed, which was followed by some stifled student laughter, and then she stepped down.

I scanned Zara's face for a reaction. She looked indifferent and continued to munch on her kabab. I smiled and asked her, "So, do you think celebrating the Mawlid is *bid'ah*?" She adjusted her glasses and shook her head, "No, but it's not for me. I'm not gonna do it, but whatever they wanna do, I don't have a problem." She paused for a second and then continued, "This is so interesting though. BU is the strangest place. They're celebrating the birth of the Prophet Muhammad. At a church. With a music group. What is that all about??" We didn't get a chance to finish our conversation because Amani joined us just then to say hello. We chatted about her classes and *halal* nail polish for a few minutes, after which we each went about our way.

Zara did not attend the actual Mawlid concert, but she clearly had strong opinions about it. During a conversation a couple of weeks later after the event had taken place, the issue of the Mawlid came up again. We were sitting in the MSA's prayer room on the newly installed red rugs, having just finished the late afternoon prayer. This time Zara recalled Zaynab's comment about it being *bid'ah* and noted, "That wasn't a very nice comment to make in a room of like . . . you don't know anyone else's perspective." I asked her what she thought of the Mawlid generally. "I stopped thinking about religion as *bid'ah* or not, for me the function of religion matters more. So, what are people getting out of this event? I don't think people are doing this to honor the Prophet or celebrate his birth; they don't even know when he was born. But I think that to gain whatever sense of religion, they feel that they need this . . . that it's good for them."

I reminded her of her comment about the celebration at a church with a music group. "Why did you say that? What did you mean by that?"

She tilted her to the left and smiled. "Look, just, with my background, being from the Indian subcontinent and having lived in the Middle East, if this happened there . . . it would be bad. And they celebrate it too; it's not like they don't. In Pakistan and some parts of India at least they do, but if you celebrated it with a musical group in a church, that's blasphemous."

I nodded, and she continued. "But I can't say that here, because then I would. . . . Yeah, people would be pretty pissed off." Why couldn't she say that here?

"Because this is trademark Bellington University. If I could describe BU, this is it. It fits right into what they believe in, what they're trying to promote."

"Which is . . . ?" I asked.

"Which is, this more inclusive view of what religion is, and bringing people together through music and events and ritual. It just doesn't make any sense. But I guess it's more about feeling, it doesn't have to make sense," she concluded.

The event, as I described at the beginning of this chapter, was held at the BU church. Returning for a moment to the significance of physical space for religious pluralism,[71] we can note that it was important for BU to host the Mawlid at the church as a marker of interfaith diversity and pluralism, even if it was not at all significant for the Muslim students. The church is best described as a larger-than-life structure, complementing the rest of the campus architecture while dominating its surroundings. The church's main auditorium is filled with stained glass windows and mosaics, with various images depicting angels, saints, Jesus, and his disciples. The performers at the Mawlid stood or sat at the chancel while the audience sat in the pews.

The program began with Amani's Qur'an recitation, followed by a speech from Zaynab, who first highlighted the RLO and its services, then the significance of the Prophet Muhammad and therefore the Mawlid. She especially pointed out the privilege of holding it at the BU church, emphasizing inclusion and diversity as core BU values. Her speech was followed by a short performance by a BU student ensemble, and the show culminated in various songs by the Sufi ensemble from Spain. BU was not the first campus at which this group was performing. Prior to their BU visit, the group had already played before audiences at two university chapels across the country, as well as at some local Muslim institutions.

They sang mostly in Arabic and English, their lyrics highlighting love, peace, devotion, and beauty. The instrumentals, composed of violin, cello, a *qanun*, and *darbukas*[72] evoked Arab, Moorish, Turkish, and Celtic tunes. They ended the performance with "Salawat"—a traditional Muslim song in praise of the Prophet Muhammad that has been performed in various languages and tunes across cultures and history. The Mawlid concert at BU was a huge success by institutional standards. RLO was quite proud of the event, and BU held another one the following year at the church, this time with a *qawwali*[73] performing group.

From the official perspective of BU, the concert checked all the boxes for active engagement with religious diversity.[74] It was, after, all, an interfaith and intercultural encounter commemorating the birth of Islam's central figure, held at an ecumenical church, with mystical music. What's not to like?

I will let my interlocutors answer that question momentarily. Before that, it is important to note that the BU Muslim Student Association (MSA) had not co-sponsored this event. It was a RLO initiative, co-sponsored by the MCC and other campus partners. It was advertised on the Muslim mailing lists, but most Muslim students I spoke with were either indifferent toward the Mawlid concert or they thought it was bizarre. Yusuf said it was a "cultural or community event" more so than an "Islamic one." He was uninterested in attending and did not go to the concert. When I asked Kareem, Khalil, and Idris about it, they were not even aware of the event and thus had not gone. Amira, who did go, found it strange but still attended and volunteered, as a courtesy to Chaplain Zaynab, with whom she had a good relationship. Amani was part of the program as she had recited the opening chapter of the Qur'an in Arabic and English to commence it. Her personal views on it, however, were unformed. When I asked about them, she told me she was aware of opposing perspectives on celebrating it, but it wasn't anything that was specifically discussed in her home when she was growing up. "It's not like my parents told us not to celebrate it, but it just never came up," she explained. Zara did not attend, and as noted above, she had strong critical views on it.

It would be reasonable to ask why the students reacted the way they did, especially those who were critical of it. The short answer is that they knew the event was not actually *for* them; that their religious difference and celebration were being used to further BU's broader pluralism project. The Mawlid concert served BU's institutional aims, bolstering its image as a secular pluralistic campus, and the Muslim students' reactions reveal the form and function of pluralism in a Protestant–secular campus context.

The longer answer, then, is that their discomfort and confusion surrounding the event indicate their recognition of some sort of imbalance around religion and religious diversity on campus. In her book *Critical Religious Pluralism in Higher Education,* Jenny Small proposes a critical theory approach to religious diversity instead of an interfaith dialogue approach. The latter, she argues, "lacks a critical awareness of power differentials between religious groups" because of its "founding and grounding in the norms and assumptions of American Christianity."[75] Such power differentials can be discerned in the Mawlid event at BU. That the event was held at BU's church evokes a metaphor for Protestant Christianity as the frame of engagement: the Christian church, quite literally, encompassed the Muslim event. We can see Chaplain Zaynab—intentionally or not—revealing this power dynamic—perhaps unknowingly -when she felt the need to emphasize that "the church is a space for everyone" when announcing the Mawlid to Muslim students, and again at the event itself when she noted that the church was "a symbol of inclusion."

The students who did attend, or who were perplexed or critical—like Amira and Zara— also alluded to the power differentials. As Amira noted, "I was looking around in there and I was like, paintings of Jesus and of saints and stuff... I was just like wow; it's come to this." Both Zara and Amira, having had transnational experience, refer to other Muslim contexts, at home in America and abroad, in the Mawlid discussion. Zara reminded me that Indians and Pakistanis, too, very much celebrate the Mawlid but not at a church, which, according to her, would be "blasphemous." Amira indicated that not only her relatives in Malaysia but also her immediate family and community in Southern California would find the event quite strange too. "I've seen our neighbors and some family celebrate it," she told me, "But it's usually more low-key like a gathering at home with ladies and food, and they recite the *Fatihah* (the opening chapter of the Qur'an)." According to her, they would find the church Mawlid "wrong in all sorts of ways."

Thus, the students *were* familiar with the Mawlid in various contexts. Amani even mentioned "Mawlid-associated sugar candy" that people made in Tanzania, where her grandparents lived. So, their reactions to the Mawlid on campus were neither a result of their unfamiliarity with the celebration itself nor something emerging out of intra-Muslim debates on its "innovation" status and validity. (Marking the birthday of Prophet Muhammad is becoming more ubiquitous among American Muslims. It is even taking off on different social media and online platforms and is transcending ethnic, cultural, and gender boundaries.)[76]

Rather, the students' reactions are indicative of their uneasiness with the juxtaposition of the Mawlid at the BU church and, by extension, their discomfort with their institution leveraging their Muslimness for its own aims. Such a pluralistic move on the institution's part was not received as such by the Muslim students who, we might reasonably expect, would be the target of such inclusion. Bender and Klassen remind us that pluralism's "historical conditions contributed to the framework wherein our understanding of pluralism (and various related ideas of multiculturalism, interfaith, and ecumenism) begins with visions of socially contained and organized encounters."[77] The BU Mawlid is a prime example of such an encounter. Ostensibly, it is not the sort of encounter that is severely oppressive to these Muslim students. However, it is one that they nevertheless find awkward or problematic because what is ordinarily a Muslim devotional ritual or commemoration—that they are actually otherwise quite familiar with—is packaged in a frame and presented in a register that is illegible to them and is, therefore, *not for them*. The Mawlid could have been held anywhere on campus, but it was held at the BU church for two consecutive years. Location aside, it was not a student-initiated or -requested event, garnering their apathy (at best) and critique (at worst). The "prescriptive pluralism" of such an interfaith encounter is exactly as Zara described: "music, events, and ritual to bring people together" as a means of inclusion to evoke the sort of "tamer spiritual expression" of religion that Protestant Christianity emphasizes.[78] Going back to discourse, students approach this event with skepticism, but none of them actually voiced their opinions because, as Zara noted, "this is trademark BU" and "people would be pretty pissed off" if she expressed how she actually felt about the event.

Conclusion: Pluralism's Power

Taken together, the above perspectives and examples at BU help us understand the institutional context within which Muslim students reside and how pluralism works at their campus. If we consider religious practice, discourse, and encounter as three (though not the only) dimensions of pluralism, what they reveal is a complex picture of engagement with religious diversity at a secular university.

To parse the complexity, let us return to Amanda Porterfield. In writing about post-secularity and pluralism on campus, Porterfield contends that religious pluralism and democracy can often be in tension. For her, the linkage between religious pluralism and democracy is problematic for two reasons—first, because religious pluralism convolutes democracy itself—which, according to her, is meant to be about protecting the rights of *individuals* and not about protecting the rights of cultural or religious *groups*. (The emphasis on individual versus groups is, in some ways, also a Protestant theme.) The second reason, and the one more relevant to our discussion here, is that "pluralism tends to lift up the best and most socially constructive aspects of religion as normative and to downplay or critique those aspects of particular religions that fall short or fail to harmonize with other religions."[79] Pluralism, says

Porterfield, has a "pro-religion" bias in that while it does not demand exclusivity to a particular religion or tradition, it "is not detached from commitment to religion as a generically good thing."[80]

My observations indicate that Porterfield's observations on pluralism and its bias pan out at BU but only partially. This is because the "religion" in "pro-religion bias" is misleading: it implies a universal category and therefore an equal bias toward all religions, whereas the privileged seat of power is not equally accessible to all religions. Instead, the central emerging theme at BU is that the "religion" in "pro-religion" is Protestant Christianity. In this way, BU, a supposedly secular institution, has a Protestant Christian bias. In terms of religious practice, it is revealed in the form of internalization by the Muslim students, who rate BU positively in its accommodation of their needs without critical consideration of enduring Christian privilege around them. In terms of religious discourse, it is revealed in their hesitation to bring up religion in conversations or classrooms, a move that not only affirms the private/public Protestant theme vis-à-vis religion but one that also preserves Protestant privilege by silencing other perspectives. And in religious encounter, the bias is more obvious in the Mawlid case study where the Muslim students are genuinely perplexed as to the form and purpose of the celebration.

Pluralism's Protestant power, therefore, lies in serving as a tenable inclusion framework while maintaining its historical legacy and status. Of late, the discourse of pluralism writ large has resurged after a tumultuous 2023–2024 academic year following student protests and increased activism surrounding the war in Gaza. Patel has continued to champion pluralism's value for higher education and college campuses, characterizing it as a lofty goal for institutions. Expanding its features beyond religious pluralism to identity pluralism, intellectual or ideological pluralism, value pluralism, and agnostic pluralism, Patel has decried the "oppressor vs. oppressed" framework as being unhelpful in diversity work.[81] Other versions of the category have also gained traction, such as Danielle Allen's "confident pluralism," which claims to uphold human rights for all and to engage productively across difference.[82] This resurgence has happened in a moment when diversity, equity, and inclusion (DEI) initiatives have come under fire[83] and academics have begun to propose, as an alternative, a pluralist framework to diversity and difference.[84]

The core problem that remains, however, is that none of these frameworks sufficiently consider power, privilege, and historical imbalances. In fact, some commentators even recommend a retreat from these considerations: "At the core of pluralistic approaches are facilitated conversations among participants with diverse identities, religious beliefs and political ideologies, but without a predetermined list of favored identities or a preconceived framework of power, privilege and oppression."[85]

To be sure, taking into consideration power, privilege, and oppression does not mean putting specific categories or communities of people into predetermined boxes. In this vein, my exposition of Muslim students' experiences of pluralism and inclusion at BU does not imply that they are oppressed. In fact, we need not deploy the "oppressor vs oppressed" binary—often a red herring—at all to understand the complexity of their experiences. Rather, my goal has been to illustrate the limits of inclusion which cannot be revealed without an acknowledgment of power and privilege. In Chapter 4 we will see how these students exercise agency and creativity to make sense of and resist institutional and paradigmatic structures within which they operate, further demonstrating that they are far from oppressed. But how can we appreciate this agency if we don't first acknowledge that there is a preexisting structural configuration set up and continually mediated by historical power and privilege?

Bender and Klassen propose that when analyzing pluralism and its specific contexts, it should be understood "as a discourse of the future that cannot escape the past."[86] In this chapter, I have attempted to draw a line from pluralism's historical past rooted in Protestantism to its present-day practice, which continues to have Protestant features that are sometimes implicit and other times explicit. These features are exposed in the experiences and perspectives of a non-Protestant community in a specific context—namely, Muslim students at a secular campus.

As a "discourse of the future," then, pluralism must contend with its own history before forging ahead. This is especially necessary in higher education, where diversity initiatives initially exploded and have now become a site of contestation, all without sufficient consideration of the paradigm within which they are conceived of, executed, and now dismantled.

Notably, Eck has touched on this issue in differentiating between inclusivism, which, according to her, is "majoritarian", and pluralism, which is transformative: "Universities, for example, are proud to admit a more diverse student body and include a more diverse group of trustees and faculty, but assume the structures of the university will not change if they do. The pluralist would insist that the shape of the table will change, the structures will change."[87] Returning to Jones's metaphorical dining table around which American religions and traditions are seated, we see that it would then not be enough for Protestant Christianity to give up the seat of power or even the shape of the table changing. Instead, we might benefit from considering whether we need to replace the table with something else altogether.[88] Klassen asks, "Can telling a new story about an old category decenter the privileges that whiteness, maleness, heterosexuality, or Christianity have bestowed on certain people and not others in North America?"[89] The case of BU would lead us to conclude—likely not. Religious pluralism is an old category about which universities such as BU are trying to tell a new story. Decentering privileges would need a critical deconstruction and then a reconstruction of a new category or, perhaps, categories. Works like Small's critical theory of religious pluralism[90] are a step in that direction, which remind us that it is not enough to point to accommodations and diversity initiatives as promoting pluralism because they continue to consider students (such as Muslim students) as *objects* of those initiatives. Instead, we might benefit more from considering students as agents, by investigating more deeply how they *receive* these pluralistic initiatives and what they might recommend instead.

3

Privatization in Public: Protestant Logics and (In)Visible Religion

> *Amani: There are things I want to talk about, like gender, race, sexuality, in relation to religion, and it's really hard to do that. Not just on campus but like even within the Muslim community here, it's almost impossible.*
>
> *Me: So, what do you do when you have something to say about these things?*
>
> *Amani: I just put it aside. Like, I don't necessarily put it aside and discard it; I mean it's put aside separately. It's still in my . . . it might be still sitting in me, but just like separately. Yeah.*

We've already seen a broad picture of Bellington University's (BU's) institutional dynamics and context vis-à-vis engaging Muslim students, which illustrates how religious pluralism at BU reproduces Protestant Christian privilege.[1] One feature of that picture is Muslim students' inability or hesitation to talk about religion in campus discourse. This reticence is based partly on their experience and understanding of the expectation that religion should be kept private and especially not inserted into discourse on sociocultural issues involving politics, gender, and race.

What happens, however, when such conversations *do* include religion? In this chapter, we move a level down from the macro, taking a meso-level public culture approach[2] to answering this question.

Being Muslim on Campus. Abiya Ahmed, Oxford University Press. © Oxford University Press 2026.
DOI: 10.1093/9780197773628.003.0004

I examine how such discourses take place and are experienced by Muslim students in intracommunity Muslim settings. Even though they do not typically encounter religion within discourse on campus broadly, they do, however, sometimes encounter it in intracommunity settings. These events are usually organized by the Religious Life Office (RLO), the Mosaic Cultural Center (MCC), the Islamic Studies program, or the Muslim Student Association (MSA), or even sometimes in classes about Islam or Muslims. In this chapter, I describe two such events: one, organized by the Islamic Studies program and hosted at the MCC; and the other, the MSA elections. Both events discuss, in different ways, the intersection of Islam and gender—the former addressing it more broadly and the latter specifically in the context of female-led prayer.

That these discourses are about gender is important. Tracy Fessenden has shown that issues of gender and specifically women's rights acutely highlight how the standard secularization narrative places Protestant freedoms on one end and "backward religions" on the other end of a civilizing scale.[3] While my research is not focused directly on the intersection of gender with Islam and Muslims, in this chapter gender politics and related discourses sharpen the focus on the public/private and liberal/conservative tensions that Muslim students face at their campus because these are sites where the tensions sharply play out.

The Islamic Studies and the MSA elections reify specific notions of religion and therefore become two ends of a liberal/conservative discursive structure rooted in Protestant–secular logics, which limit the possible ways in which students engage with Islam or their Muslimness. Ironically, while both events make public opposing positions on the issue of Islam and gender—liberal and conservative, respectively—the outcome of both events for my interlocutors is the same: privatization of their own religious beliefs and perspectives. In offering these Muslim students a binary structure within which to engage their Islam and Muslimness, what BU and its institutional substructures actually do is lead them to keep their own Islamic beliefs, ideas, and questions private.

As an original feature of secularity, privatization is now considered untenable by scholars of religion.[4] Building on this foregone conclusion, scholars at the intersection of religion and higher education point to that detail when asserting that the academy is in a postsecular age where religion is no longer concealed and must be engaged.[5] What is remarkable is that the literature on religion on campus is almost always about *religion* (singular) on campus and rarely about *religions* (plural) on campus, conceptually speaking. I have detailed the difference extensively in Chapter 1, but it bears repeating here: religion (singular) is a category with a Protestant genealogy, which constructs a universal definition of religion to mean something that is private, voluntary, individual, textual, and believed.[6] The plural—religions—would imply more than one definition. I stress this point because when Jacobsen and Jacobsen note, for example, that "religion is no longer invisible," which and whose religion are they referring to? Is it possible that one version of religion might be visible and another version invisible? I maintain that it is possible, a position I illustrate through the case of Muslim students for whom the available discourses on religion fall short of meeting their ideas about religion. This is because the discursive structures within which these students encounter religion limit their choices about how to discuss and engage religion. The outcome of that limitation is privatization on their part.

This chapter is therefore organized as follows: first, I explain what the overarching discursive structure is and how that structure is represented by the two events. Then, I describe the events and how the Muslim students experience them, followed by an analysis of why the outcome of this experience leads them to privatize their own beliefs. I end by discussing what we can learn from religious privatization vis-à-vis Muslims and the imposition of binary categories on them.

Campus Discursive Structure

In my discussion of the overarching discursive structure on campus, I draw from Jakobsen and Pellegrini's extrapolation of the religious–secular and public–private binary rooted in Protestant secularism, especially as it relates to Islam and Muslims. They note that while the religious right and the secular left have starkly opposite positions on whether or not the public sphere should be completely secular, they actually agree that:

> [c]ivilization can be found in Europe and [the] US, while Islam, particularly when not contained in the private sphere, threatens civilization and leads to violence. *This consensus between left and right produces a rhetorical structure with only a limited number of positions.* Liberal advocates of religion, for example, are left with the choice of either siding with secularists, who deny the import of religion to public life, or with conservative Christians, who admit religion to public life but deny the import of liberal values to religion.[7]

As Jakobsen and Pellegrini note, the Protestant genealogy of secularity has much to do with the production of this rhetorical structure, which inevitably exists in various institutional contexts, including mainstream media, civil life, the market, *and* college campuses.[8] That the consensus happens around Islam/Muslims is a significant consideration and one that has been articulated more comprehensively in the context of American Islamophobia.[9] Delving into it deeply is beyond the scope of this book, but the result of that consensus—that is, a limited number of choices—is critical to understanding why conventional narratives of religion in higher education do not always neatly apply to Muslim students. More specifically, the campus discourses on Islam described below *reproduce* the "rhetorical structure" that Jakobsen and Pellegrini refer to, such that there are only two evident choices for Muslim students: to align with either the liberal secular left or the religious right.

In the BU context, the liberal secular left position is represented by the "Gender in the American Muslim context" event that I describe below, organized by the Islamic Studies program and hosted at the MCC. As discussed previously, the place of religion on campus in terms of the Religious Studies discipline and extracurricular activities is entangled with a Protestant–secular history and bias. Religious Studies reproduces Protestant–secular notions of religion,[10] and we can see how that trickles down at an event discussing gender and Islam. With regard to extracurriculars, students are embedded in a "contested secular ethos" in which campus diversity efforts may legitimize their religious identity but fail to account for the fact that their "questions about privatized religion can challenge campus secular norms."[11] The events I describe in this chapter occur in conditions that adhere to certain norms, which ultimately impact how the students respond to them.

The opposite end of the discursive structure is represented by the MSA elections. I am not suggesting here that the BU MSA is wholly and entirely representative of the "religious right" as conceived in the Jakobsen and Pellegrini model. Rather, what I am positing is that on this particular issue—Islam and gender—the discourses that I describe reify religion in a different way, thus representing a choice that is starkly opposed to the one in the Islamic Studies event but a limiting one nevertheless.

MSAs, Revivalism, and Secularism

To understand this discursive structure further, a brief history of the Muslim Student Associations (MSAs) is helpful. the founding of MSAs in American higher education coincides with the rise of postmodernism, the civil rights movement, and the influx of immigrants from Muslim countries in the 1960s. The first MSA was founded in 1963 at the University of Illinois at Urbana-Champaign. In the earlier years, most members were male students studying engineering and medicine with affiliations to pan-Islamic groups such as the Muslim Brotherhood in Egypt or the Jama'at-i-Islami in Pakistan.[12] The implication of these affiliations was not that these students blindly followed or approved of all these groups' activities or that there was some sort of foreign allegiance, but rather that they "saw themselves as participants in a historical Islamic 'renaissance' ushered in by such Islamist thinkers as Abul A'la Mawdudi and Sayyid Qutb, the contemporary ideologues of Jam'at-i-Islami and the Muslim Brotherhood." Put simply, the MSA was meant to be a mechanism for realizing a "utopian" understanding of Islam as a "complete way of life" in the United States.[13]

Recent research by Justine Howe has also shown how the MSA Women's Committee—then a subentity under the national MSA—contributed to revivalist goals through publications on parenting, family dynamics, and cooking.[14] Howe examines the literature produced by MSA female members between 1963 and 1980 to illustrate how these writings were a "critique of American society as excessively consumerist and sexually licentious" as well as "predicated on the conviction that the United States was an especially promising site for Muslim reform and renewal."[15] Thus, the American context was and continues to be critical in the development of MSAs, especially in terms of their extracurricular activity on and beyond campus.

Today, there are more than 500 MSA chapters across the United States and Canada,[16] and the MSA membership demographics and priorities have changed. Notably, most members are American-born Muslims whose priority is "learning how to integrate and institutionalize Islam into American society and culture."[17] Female participation too, has come a long way from producing parenting and cookbook manuals to appointing the first female MSA National president in 2004.

Still, the revivalist impulse persists. However, it persists not in terms of pan-Islamic political affiliations but in terms of essentializing Muslim practice and defining Islam. On gender, for example, Shabana Mir has noted how MSAs often "employ stricter 'Islamic' gendered practices than most Muslims practice in their personal lives," which serves the purpose of differentiating Muslims as Muslims on campus and providing "leadership, community, and religious frameworks to Muslims."[18]

If revivalism and the imperative to define, preserve, and practice Islam in particular ways represent one leg of MSAs' religious framework, the other leg is a "rhetorical opposition to Western secularism"[19] as indicated by the MSAs' positioning, patterns, and practices in both historical and contemporary contexts.[20] This continnum positioning revivalism and antisecularism as polar opposities is actually quite ironic because, as Zaid Adhami has argued:

> . . . revivalism and secularism are similar in that they are both ideological projects aimed at making "religion" more visible and clearly demarcated in society—the former to make it more influential, authentic, and purified, and the latter to restrict its influence in society. The impulse in both secularism and revivalism to clearly identity, reify, and objectify a "religion" has similar causes and implications.[21]

What this means, for our purposes, is that the revivalist framework of the MSA is not that different from the secularism it sets itself against because both of them promote certain ideas about religion. Moreover, the irony of the revivalist paradigm in this campus context is that it results in the very same outcome that it set out to contest: namely, privatization of religion. What I mean here, and as will become clear, is that Muslim students at BU like neither their "liberal secular" option (in the form of the Islamic Studies event) nor their "conservative revivalist" option (in the form of MSA elections). Because they are uncomfortable with both options, Muslim students keep their own ideas about religion private during these respective discourses.

Disruption vs. Privatization

In *Formations of the Secular,* Talal Asad asks: "If adherents of a religion enter the public sphere, can their entry leave the preexisting discursive structure intact?"[22] He asks this question in the context of nation-states and the "public sphere" writ large, but it can be asked similarly of campus discourses conducted in an intracommunity setting, especially for a residential institution such as BU where students' lives are embedded on campus. Asad continues:

> The public sphere is not an empty space for carrying out debates. It is constituted by the sensibilities—memories and aspirations, fears and hopes—of speakers and listeners. And also by the manner in which they exist (and are made to exist) for each other, and by their propensity to act or react in distinctive ways. Thus, the introduction of new discourses may result in the disruption of established assumptions structuring debates in the public sphere. More strongly: they may *have* to disrupt existing assumptions to be heard.[23]

When Muslim students at BU encounter public discourse on religion, they automatically enter into a discursive structure built on assumptions embedded in the campus institutional context generally and in the subcontext of an event specifically. These assumptions are rooted in Protestant–secular logics of the private–public, religious–secular, liberal–conservative binary, which leaves students with two choices. While these choices might work for some students, they leave out others like Amani who might more accurately describe themselves as liberal advocates of religion, whose lived experience and engagement of Islam are more complex than what the structure offers. If students like Amani are to be heard and their perspectives are to be taken seriously by the institution or substructures within the institution, they would have to *disrupt* the discursive structure. But they do not; instead, they opt out of engaging with the discourse and decide to keep their ideas private. The limitations of such a discursive structure explain why the Muslim students in my study find it difficult to articulate their own religious perspectives or questions, which ultimately means that *their* version of religion, or at least some parts of it, is invisible, even if *a* version of religion is visible "out there" in a given space and event.

Gender in the American Muslim Context

A couple of weeks after the Mawlid concert, another "Muslim-related" event was held at BU. This event took place at the intersection of gender and activism in the American Muslim context. It was part of an "Islam in America" series sponsored by the BU Islamic Studies program and co-sponsored by the Religious Life Office (RLO) as well as the Mosaic Cultural Center (MCC).

Structured in the form of a panel discussion, the event featured Talia O'Keefe, an African American convert to Islam who had been involved in one of the women's mosques in the United States. Other speakers were Chaplain Zaynab from RLO and Roya Ghorbani, a junior Religious Studies scholar at a liberal arts college. The discussion was held at the MCC space and moderated by Melanie Wright from the Islamic Studies program.[24]

I arrived early in time to grab some dinner, but as the event was open to the public, the room filled up quickly. I made myself a plate and found a spot in the front row, with a clear view of where the speakers were seated. The MCC space could hold about forty to fifty people, and pretty soon there was standing room only. Amani had joined me in the front on a couch right next to the chairs. Just as the discussion was beginning, I spotted and smiled at Ayesha in the audience, who smiled back and waved at me.

Once people settled down, Melanie introduced the speakers and said they would each have ten minutes to address the question of what diversity in Muslim spaces means to them, after which there would be questions. Talia—dressed in blue jeans and a black top with a Spanish or turban-style hijab wrap, bright lipstick, and dark eyeliner—began the conversation. Her main point was that the primary barrier to diversity in Muslim spaces was gender segregation propagated by "an all-male leadership model, which is entirely a religious model, where politics and social justice have no place." She spoke firmly and loudly:

> We need to stop women from being space-less, faceless, formless. We need to include female prophets, we need to stop referring to God as a man, God is not a man! God is an Energy, a Creative Force. We need female imams, trans, gay imams. We need to stop relying on the Arab model of Islam, on Hadith, because Hadith are often misogynist, racist, and backward.

As Amani was right next to me, I observed her while Talia spoke, and I could sense some discomfort as her body shifted slightly every now and then and she took deep breaths, especially at the last bit about Hadiths. I tilted my head slightly to look at Ayesha, who, with her eyes wide and lips pursed, looked visibly disturbed. Talia spoke some more, and at one point during her talk she casually took off her hijab. (She later explained she had done that to illustrate that it was okay to do so.)

Next, Roya introduced herself with the caveat that she approached the question as an academic. Her central argument was one about interpretation. "We hear people say Islam says this or Islam is this, but Islam is nothing. No religion is anything. All we are dealing with is interpretation." She brought up the interpretations of Amina Wadud, an African American Muslim scholar of Islam, who, in 2005, led the first and highly controversial female-led Friday prayer in New York. "So, do we accept that as authentic?" she asked. "I personally like the model of Imam Da'ee Abdullah, whose mosque is all-inclusive, and he himself is gay, he performs marriage and funeral rituals for gays," she added.

When she was done, Zaynab introduced herself as the Muslim chaplain at BU and as being affiliated with RLO. She not only addressed the upward challenge for women but also touched upon figures whom she considered female role models in Islam: "According to me, Maryam, Mary the mother of Jesus, is a prophet. She communicated with God." She also mentioned Umm Waraqah, a female contemporary of the Prophet Muhammad who, according to Zaynab, used to recite the Qur'an out loud and whose recitation he did not stop but rather encouraged.

Zaynab did not take up much time, so Melanie allowed the speakers to engage with each other briefly before opening it up for Q&A. The first question, asked by an elderly gentleman, was directed at Talia; he asked her about her conversion to Islam, which she addressed briefly as being a result of being influenced by the Sufi Naqshabandi order. After him, a woman, who presumably had a question, spoke for almost five minutes about her perspective on the issue. Her short sermon was laced with statements such as "All religions are the same," "All God wants is for you to be good person," and "Forget about Hadith, I don't follow it." As she spoke, Zaynab tried to get Melanie's attention to interrupt. Amani continued to shift in her seat uncomfortably; at one point she looked at me and shook her head in disbelief. Since Melanie did not seem to see the need to interrupt, finally Zaynab interrupted the woman, asking if she had a question. She didn't.

Another gentleman said he wanted to comment on what had been said. He began to note that Islam, unlike other religions, had no clergy and that the speakers on stage were complicating matters by mixing Western cultural influences with religion. "It's between you and God, like she said [referring to the woman who spoke just before him]. If you understand anything else, then you're missing the essence of Islam."

At this point, Roya interrupted him to say, "I have a question. What *is* the essence of Islam?"

"The essence of Islam is between you and God. Your worship is a private affair between you and God. It has nothing to do with whether you're straight or gay or anything and all of you are mixing up things by bringing in—."

Talia interrupted him right then, "Here is a classic example of a man taking up space." He started to disagree, at which point she interrupted him again to exclaim, "EXCUSE ME! You are NOT going to be the one to tell three intelligent women up here what they are saying! You are not going to tell me what to think or what I know!" At this point, there was palpable silence in the room.

Before things spiraled further out of control, Zaynab, seeking to calm the atmosphere, took over the facilitation and asked, "Are there any students with any questions?" None of the earlier questioners or commentators had been students, and no one raised their hand even now. Amani was looking around nervously at the audience, and Ayesha was looking at her phone. Finally, Melanie took one more question (not from a student) and then formally concluded the event.

As the audience dispersed and began conversing, I turned to Amani. She whispered immediately, "What was that??! I'm having like a physical reaction to this, I'm shaking right now. This event has totally disturbed me." I nodded in empathy, "It's okay, take it easy," I told her. Before I could say anything else, Zaynab walked over to us while looking around the audience, her eyes searching for someone. "I saw Ayesha walk out earlier, she looked traumatized, I just wanted to speak to her before she left," she explained. We all walked toward the exit, and I told Amani, "Get some rest. We'll talk about this later."

We did pick up on it a few days after, when Amani and I were seated in the Student Center in a more relaxed setting. It was late

Friday afternoon; prayers had ended, and we were the only ones there. The space was dark and cool, and we had found ourselves a quiet spot by the wall with cushions to rest on. Amani had much to share that day; she had warned me before I pressed record.

"Where do you want to begin? You said you have a lot of thoughts . . ." I asked.

"I mean, I don't even know if they're thoughts. I was *very* overwhelmed during that gender event. I was like, 'I wanna dip now.' There was a lot happening and for many different reasons I feel like first, the moderator did not do her job. Like 'Moderator, do your job!' And then, also the space, even though Marissa [the MCC manager] had warned that the space wasn't necessarily more conducive to that event, and I felt like there was some crowding of sorts, which I guess is minor. But it all adds. And then, even moderating the Q&A. . . ." She sighed and then continued, "I feel like there was a lot that could have been done to make it a very productive discussion. I was very excited for it. I was looking for tools to have a productive conversation, and then suddenly I was like, 'Oh my gosh, I gotta go now, this is very overwhelming.'"

I let her words sit for a few seconds and then I asked, "Tell me, apart from the physical and logistical aspect of it, what in particular bothered you?"

"There was no nuance," she replied right away, "A lot of things were just being said with no nuance, no explanation, and no backing."

"Can you think of particular comments that were made?" I probed.

"Yeah, the dissing of the Hadith, 100% I was just like, "What?"! See, here's the thing, it's like, okay, yes, I believe that the concept of interpretation is very important when looking at these things. I do, and I'm becoming more in-tune with that, and I'd like to do more learning and more research. But the way it was discussed was like . . . anybody can say anything. But if you're not discussing it with nuance and you're not giving examples, what's the point? You can *literally* say *anything*, it doesn't make it right or wrong. So, at this point, I really don't care."

"You don't care?"

"I mean I still care about gender issues; it's just I don't care about the way they are being spoken of, in this context. I mean, if you're going to be radical, if you're going to question [the] status quo, do it in a way that's productive, right? The event turned me off very much. So, I was like, 'I'm just gonna stick to what my parents taught me.'"

Amani was clearly disturbed by what had been said, but she was more bothered by how the conversation had been handled and the manner in which the discourse took place. She wasn't the only one who felt that way. As Zaynab had correctly observed, Ayesha, too, had been impacted by the event. In one interview with her not long after the event, Ayesha told me she was intrigued by the event when it was first advertised. "I said to myself, 'I should go. I should challenge my viewpoint, that's what college is all about,'" she recalled. By that Ayesha meant that her own views on gender were on the traditional end, and she was expecting the event to be on the liberal end, but she was interested to engage.

"And were you challenged?" I asked.

"Well, for one thing, the woman in the middle, I forgot her name, [Roya] was very academic, and she, I think she tried to emphasize that point, but what I realized was that she wasn't really basing stuff in Islam that much. And really what bothered me so much was while we were at the event, and nobody stopped to pray *Maghrib* [the sunset prayer]. I went to go pray and I was like, 'This is an event talking about women leading prayer and no one cares enough to even make time to pray, so why are we even having this discussion?' And that's when I realized, this is all . . . this is mainly political and it's not Islamic, and that . . . it really bothered me," Ayesha explained.

"I see," I responded.

Ayesha continued, "And then the woman on the left [Talia], who was very . . . more liberal minded, she was going all off against every Islamic thing, she was like, 'I can pray when I'm on my period,' and 'I can take this hijab off when I want.' So, everything about that was the opposite of submitting to God, which is what Islam is about. She was saying, 'When I want to do something, I'm going to do it, and nobody can tell me not to.' But no, that's not what Islam is."

"What about Zaynab?"

"Zaynab, I don't think she actually specifically spoke on women leading. But she did say something, which I actually did appreciate. She mentioned the one thing that had [an] Islamic background. She mentioned the story of the woman who had, at the time of the Prophet, who would recite the Qur'an really loudly, and one day she didn't, and the Prophet went to her home to check on her. And so, the reason she brought that up was to [note] . . . as a piece of evidence that women can recite out loud. And I actually appreciated that because it . . . she was like using something from Islam."

Ayesha and I discussed what she meant by "from Islam," which, for her, revolved around the Qur'an, Hadiths, and legitimate Islamic scholarship. I address these three factors in depth in the next chapter, but here it is useful to note that Ayesha felt the discourse was generally not grounded in what she considered authentic Islam. The event itself and my subsequent conversations with the BU community led me to wonder the following: if students found the content and structure so disturbing, why didn't any of them say something *during* the event? "It just wasn't conducive to saying anything." Amani explained to me: "there was no room to even breathe, much less voice some kind of dissent." Ayesha's response was that the event had been organized by the Religious Studies Department, and, according to her, "Religious Studies programs aim to reform and change things, so when you look at Islamic Studies programs, they're more interested in what liberals typically pressure people to change their views on." She also thought the physical location of the event played a role, "The MCC is a secular space, so hot topics can't be rooted in Islam."

In addition to Ayesha and Amani, many others found the incident fraught and disturbing. I heard about it from other Muslim students, and Marissa confirmed this disquiet too, noting that her office the day after the event was "a revolving door" through which students were constantly moving both in and out, voicing their grievances about the event. Their comments were similar: it was not a productive discourse, and it made the space uncomfortable. In other words, students did have a lot to say on the issue, but they did not feel comfortable enough to say it in public; rather, they felt an intimate conversation with close friends or supportive staff was easier. Thus, instead of engaging their perspectives on Islam and gender *at* the event, these students opted to privatize their views.

Privatization on the Liberal End

If we unpack the event, its discourse, and how students encountered it, we will understand that students like Amani and Ayesha privatize their views because of two interrelated reasons: the framing and location of the event and the discursive structure of the remarks. Both of these aspects underscore the dissonance between the students' version of religion and the event's version of it, which ultimately explains their privatization.

Although students were aware of the event's framing and location even before it took place, neither the framing nor the location initially represented a deterrent for them. In fact, they were enthusiastic and expecting to hear some contentious views and debate, but, as Amani noted, they were also "looking for the tools to have a productive conversation" on the issue of Islam and gender. Ayesha had explicitly stated, "I should challenge my viewpoint, that's what college is all about." Both of them came to the event with the intention to engage, and both of them left disturbed, as did several others. Given their enthusiasm prior to the event and knowing them to be otherwise confident in articulating their views, I had asked them why they did not engage during the event if they were so troubled by it. In their answers, we see elements of their awareness of the assumptions embedded in the discursive structure and the rules of engagement within such a structure.[25]

Before delving further into the analysis, however, allow me a brief tangent to underline the point that I am not concerned here with the issue of gender justice and Islam or with evaluating the merits of arguments in favor of or against female leadership. Numerous scholars have already analyzed these issues. For example, Juliane Hammer explains how the 2005 female-led prayer by Amina Wadud was "more than a prayer"; instead, it was an avenue for fierce contestations on issues of gender, authenticity, and tradition.[26]Additionally, as Jonathan Brown notes on the same issue, a practice's ubiquity or lack thereof within the Muslim historical tradition is, on its own, not enough to insist on a firm position on its legality or permissibility; but because the issue of female-led prayer is tied up in "the knot of gender and power," it has become controversial.[27]

What I am primarily concerned with, then, in describing this campus event, is to illustrate how the discursive structure within which the issue of gender is addressed leads some Muslim students to further privatize their religious views and questions instead of engaging them. Thus, to this "knot of gender and power" I would add the element of secularity on campus, which, in its biases not just about *what* religion is but also *when* religion is (public), privileges and makes visible a particular discourse on Islam. If we adopt Jacobsen and Jacobsen's model,[28] we can point to such an event and assert that BU is in the pluriform stage where religion is public and is not relegated to private realms. At the institutional level, we may concede that might be the case. However, at the student level, students' own ideas, beliefs, and even questions about Islam in fact *do* remain in their private realms, and thus invisible.

Why does this happen? As I noted above, it has to do with who organized the event and where it was held, as well as with the content of the remarks and how they were handled. More significantly, what the institution or its substructures make public about Islam and Muslims (and how, where, and when they make it public) does not necessarily align with the experience of Islam and Muslimness by Muslim students at that very institution.

To begin, the event was organized and hosted by the BU Islamic Studies program. As noted earlier, the discipline of Religious Studies brings with it significant Protestant Christian baggage in terms of how religion is construed as an object of study.[29] Such endurance is evident in Roya's preface to her remarks, where she noted that she would approach the topic "as an academic" and she followed that comment with statements such as "Islam is nothing. No religion is anything. All we are dealing with is interpretation." These statements, combined with Talia's and audience comments such as Islam being a "private matter between you and God" and that all one needed to be is a "good person" reinforced a particular idea of religion as being individual, private, and believed, all of which are Protestant features.[30]

On the student side, the discussion's framing and location played a role in how they understood the discourse. Ayesha, for example, believed that the academic perspective on Islam in the form of Religious Studies programs "aims to reform and change things" and that Islamic Studies in this context was more about succumbing to liberal pressure. With regard to the physical location, she said that "[t]he MCC is a secular space, so hot topics can't be rooted in Islam." Ayesha felt the event sponsors, the space where it was held, the choice of speakers, and the content of the discussion were all meant to serve liberal aims without room for alternate perspectives. She did indeed have a different perspective, but she did not feel comfortable articulating it. She was also "bothered" that while the speakers were concerned with female leadership of prayer, no one actually took a break to perform the sunset prayer (she herself did;

indeed, she stepped out during the event to go pray). To her, this implied that the event "was mainly political and it's not Islamic." For Ayesha, then, the event was a site for the demarcation of the religious and the secular, the Islamic and the political, as she had pointed out. The event, she added, could have made more room not only for theoretical perspectives that she felt were "grounded in Islam"—such as Zaynab's reference to a Hadith, which she did highlight—but also for the lived/ritual aspect of it by taking a break for the sunset prayer. Ayesha's own version of religion (Islam) was not demarcated into the binaries she described, but being aware of the boundaries delineated and reinforced at the event, she opted to not cross or even blur them publicly.

In addition to the event's sponsors and location and what these meant for the ensuing discussion, the students did not articulate their views because they felt they would "disrupt" the dominant liberal frame of the discourse. Of the BU Muslim students I spent considerable amount of time with, Ayesha was one of the more traditional ones. We could attribute her discomfort to that perspective, but even Amani—with an "I'm a Feminist" decal on her MacBook and a "down with the patriarchy" agenda—felt the discourse was troubling. Amani was troubled not just by moderator failure but also by Talia's specific comments, such as Talia's unequivocal rejection of Hadith as well as her demonstration of taking off her hijab to make a point. Amani's version of religion (Islam) made room for interpretation, as she told me, but not for unchecked interpretation, with no deference to some sort of authority or nuance. If authority and nuance were deemed unimportant and unnecessary, then she pointed out, anyone "can *literally* say *anything*, it doesn't make it right or wrong." Such a subjective, individual version of religion did not make sense to her.

Amani also thought the moderator had failed to allow a productive discussion, giving too much weight to one particular perspective even if it was articulated by different people. Interestingly, even though there was obvious disagreement between Talia and one of the audience members, Amani felt they were all articulating the same perspective on Islam. From the students' vantage point, Talia, Roya, and the audience members were essentially on the liberal, secular, leftist end of the rhetorical structure that Jakobsen and Pellegrini describe.[31] This does not mean that students like Ayesha or Amani were on the other end (the religious right) because, as we will see in this chapter, the MSA elections pose similar problems for them. But they were certainly in a predicament because they could neither publicly argue against the panel's perspective nor agree with it. In this way, the event successfully reproduced the "rhetorical structure" rooted in Protestant–secularity, leaving the students no choice but to privatize and perhaps revert to what they already knew and what was familiar or comfortable for them. As Amani told me later, "I'm just going to stick to what my parents taught me." The "preexisting discursive structure" at this event and the "propensity to act or react"—especially in the Q&A session—did not give them permission to enter this debate without disrupting "existing authority" and "established assumptions."[32] Since they did not feel empowered to disrupt, they kept their perspectives private.

This particular event is thus an example of one of the limited choices available to Muslim students on campus when they are engaging in matters relating to their religious beliefs and views. In fact, as we have seen, neither Ayesha nor Amani—or any students for that matter—asked any questions during the event. Because they did not like the choice available to them and the discursive structure did not permit them to disrupt it by voicing their inquiry or disagreement, they adopted privatization as a strategy to deal with that. In the next section, I describe the opposite choice that, ironically, leads to the same outcome.

MSA Elections and Friday Prayer

Earlier that year (before this gender event), I was at the MCC one evening, where there was standing room only. I had been to several

MSA events, but this was one of the largest crowds I'd seen. It was so well attended because MSA elections were being held, with not just board positions but also constitutional amendments at stake. The most controversial of these amendments? Female-led Friday prayer (*jummah*) on campus.

One of the two MSA co-presidents, Ahmad, began the event, explaining the agenda, format, and voting process, ending his introduction by reminding everyone to be "respectful" and to recognize that "we are all Muslim here." Ahmad's preamble foreshadowed some contentious exchanges because eight of the twelve amendments were related to the Friday congregational prayer, some explicitly (and others implicitly) about women's involvement in it: where they stood to pray (the amendment proposed they pray next to the men as opposed to behind them); MSA encouragement for them to offer the sermon and lead prayers; and an amendment that the MSA would officially promote such an alternate female-led Friday prayer.

Iman, who had proposed the four amendments in favor of women leading and conducting sermons, presented her case first. Speaking gently but firmly, she noted that the "spirit of these amendments was more inclusion for women" and that since the women-led prayers had been in place, women turnout had increased. She mentioned the women's mosques of Los Angeles and Berkeley and described how these kinds of inclusive spaces "worldwide" were helping Muslim women.

A couple of students spoke out in support of Iman's propositions, but she received pushback from others (mostly male students). When she was done with the first four amendments, Haaris, the former *jummah* coordinator, presented his amendment, which basically countered all of Iman's amendments. He proposed that the MSA should hold and advertise a primary (male-led) *jummah* per the practice and consensus "agreed upon by the major Muslim schools of *fiqh* [jurisprudence]." He contended, "Even during the time of the Prophet (peace be upon him), people had very intense differences with each other—who were Muslims themselves, but during *jummah* there was a time to put aside those differences and get together for the sake of worship. And one of the things I was thinking about is that from the time of the Prophet, until now, if you were to go almost anywhere in the world to any *masjid* [mosque], you could participate in *jummah*, because the way it is done is something that has been consistent for us."

When he was done, Ahmad allowed questions or comments. Unsurprisingly, Iman raised her hand. "Is there anything in the Qur'an that specifically prohibits women from giving *khutbahs* [sermons] or lead prayer?" she asked.

Haaris responded, "My understanding is that the Prophet (peace be upon him) taught us to do it in the way that it's been done."

Iman started to respond to him, but another male student cut into the conversation, addressing Iman directly to ask: "Was the Prophet (peace be upon him) inclusive or not?"

"He was," she said confidently, "and I don't think he stopped women from—" she tried to continue but was cut off again.

"Did the Prophet (peace be upon him) allow women to lead prayer or give *khutbah*?" The same male student asked.

"Yes, he did, and—." Iman tried to continue.

"Can you tell us your reference?" He cut her off again.

"Sure, I can send it to you," she replied.

"No, no—right now!" He insisted.

"I don't have it right now," Iman responded, visibly exasperated. At this point, Ahmad stopped the exchange with a firm, "Alright we're going to end there."

The exchange ended, but students' murmurs continued until Ahmad had to get everyone's attention again, after which the elections proceeded with other agenda items. Ultimately, Iman's amendments did not pass, and Haaris's amendment did. This meant that the female-led Friday prayer that had been in place that academic year was voted out, and the following year there was no such option. Instead, the MSA continued to advertise and hold two Friday prayers at different times, both led by males.

This particular MSA election was memorable enough that students continued to talk about it long after the occurrence. It came up both in some of the formal interviews I conducted with my key interlocutors and in casual conversation with other Muslim students. Its news traveled far and wide even to students like Ayesha who had not even enrolled when they happened.

My conversations with students about these elections revealed that regardless of where students stood on the actual issue (i.e., whether or not female-led prayer was acceptable), they were generally in agreement that the elections did not offer a productive space or method of addressing the issue. As Amani, who was present at the elections, once said to me, "I still have PTSD from that day!" She added, "Look I don't know where I stand on that [female-led prayer], but I know some community members liked coming to that. And if that's one space that we could offer to people to come in, that's better than nothing I think." Amani said she would have wanted to keep the alternate female-led prayer in place, even if she herself would not attend. Amira was more assertive in her criticism and called the interaction between Iman and the male students "misogynistic." She continued, "And then people wonder why aren't more girls involved with the MSA? Well, if they're making institutional decisions and having interactions like these, then where is my place in the community? I think the MSA feels like there's a cookie-cutter kind of way of being Muslim, and they look for that and support that."

Zara said she would not attend a female-led Friday prayer but called the elections "horrible and childish." She thought the MSA needed to acknowledge an "ideological divide" in the community and conduct discourse accordingly. Yusuf, who was on the MSA board that year, described the elections as "very sad" and "poorly handled." He told me he was "on one side of the issue" and did not think women could lead Friday prayer from a juristic perspective, but he did believe there needed to be acknowledgment that some community members might be alienated for a variety of reasons.

He had proposed to the MSA board that a townhall be held to discuss the issue. "We need to have more room to just talk about it, no votes or amendments or one-minute time limits for comments, just people coming to discuss both sides of the issue," he said. During my fieldwork, no such townhall ever took place.

However, Yusuf's assessment of the need to make space for discourse was perceptive, because the issue came up again in the MSA elections the following year. This time, the amendment stated, "Bring back the co-ed *jummah*." Iman was not present, and the amendment had been proposed by another female student—Ghada, an Arab American senior. The discussion this year was less tense and more civil, centered primarily around whether or not the MSA could *officially* support a co-ed *jummah*. Saleh, one of the co-presidents leading the meeting, noted as he announced the amendment that the MSA constitution actually did not prevent anyone from holding any Friday prayer as they saw fit. A female student asked for clarification, "Would that then be under the heading of the MSA?"

"So that's the thing—no. It would be any 'interested community members' essentially doing that," Saleh explained. Haaris, present again this year, commented, "Our constitution notes that we will organize Friday prayers in accordance with the major bodies of *fiqh* [jurisprudence]." Saleh nodded and then said, "Let's hear from the supporter of this amendment."

Taking that as her cue, Ghada stood up to say, "I just think it's important to acknowledge that adding spaces where other spaces already exist is *not* preventing anyone from practicing their faith in the way that they see fit. It's just making sure that people who want to feel included in a different way have the space in which to do that. . . . And the idea should be that it doesn't need to happen under a *separate* subset of Muslim students on campus. The MSA on campus should represent the diverse set of views that people hold, which means that when somebody decides to start a co-ed *jummah*, they should have the backing of the organization to do so, because ultimately it is serving at least part of the community."

A male student spoke, "The question is how would this be implemented?" Saleh addressed this question briefly, noting that the language of the proposed amendment—"Bring back the co-ed *jummah*"—made it difficult to determine the specifics of executing it. There was silence for a few seconds, after which another female student raised her hand. Saleh called on her, and she noted, "My understanding is that the prayer can happen, but MSA can't have anything to do with it. Is that right?" Saleh nodded.

At this point, Ghada stood up and spoke again, slightly exasperated but maintaining composure, "Look, when I submitted it, I just needed a place to voice this thought. I didn't mean for it to be an amendment necessarily, but I needed a space to have this discussion."

"That's why we put it up—for transparency," Saleh replied, "because the community should be aware it's a concern. The problem is that now we don't know how it would be implemented since the specifics are unclear, and it would become an interpretive problem."

There was significant murmuring then, with several students commenting to each other. The rest of the meeting had to proceed, so Saleh urged everyone to vote on the amendments before they moved to the board elections. When results were announced later, this particular amendment did not pass.

Privatization on the Conservative End

The MSA elections present an intracommunity public discourse on Islam and gender during which students like Amani privatize their religious beliefs and views. In other words, in this setting too, a version of religion is visible and dominates, making little room for alternative perspectives, especially in the first elections. Even though this event and its discourse do not carry with it the disciplinary baggage of an "academic" Islamic Studies panel, they do reveal a different kind of baggage that the BU MSA carries and perpetuates, which has some bearing on the form and function of the discourses in which students engage.

As noted above, as a national organization, the MSA's history is rooted in the revivalist impulse,[33] which persists in some form today and is acutely evident when it comes to gender where strict lines are drawn between what is acceptable and what is not.[34] We see evidence of this impulsein the BU MSA elections I describe above, when male students like Haaris and the interrupting student insisted that Iman offer some sort of Qur'anic or Prophetic reference for the legitimacy of female-led prayer. Haaris also consistently referred to "major bodies of *fiqh*" and historical practice as sources upon which the BU MSA predicates its Friday prayer practice, implying that that was the religious framework within which the MSA operates.

In this way, revivalism, too, like secularity, reifies a particular notion of religion[35] that we might place on the "religious right" end of Jakobsen and Pellegrini's discursive structure.[36] In the BU MSA context, this perspective is perhaps best exemplified in Amira's statement, "I think the MSA feels like there's a cookie-cutter kind of way of being Muslim, and they look for that and support that." She felt she did not fit the "cookie-cutter" version and eventually resigned from her position on the MSA board, as did Amani. The outcome of such reification is, once again, that students like Amani keep their beliefs private.

Privatization in a Muslim revivalist context is actually quite ironic because revivalism, in setting itself up against secularism, actually rejects religious privatization. However, because revivalism (in this case reflected in the MSA's discourse), like secular liberalism (reflected in the gender panel), imposes a particular version of religion, privatization is *precisely* what students like Amani and Amira resort to when they do not find the MSA's discursive structure conducive to their views.

Returning to Asad and the "preexisting discursive structure,"[37] the assumptions within the MSA elections discourse are that religion (Islam) is textual and reliant on the Qur'an, Hadith, and an authoritative legal tradition. What is fascinating about the discourse is that Iman actually attempted to disrupt the structure by operating *within* those assumptions: she questioned if the Qur'an explicitly forbids female-led prayer, and when she was referred to the practice of the Prophet Muhammad, she pointed out his inclusivity in allowing women to lead prayer. Because she was unable to provide a textual reference at that very moment, her comments were dismissed. In the second elections, Ghada made a similar attempt to disrupt the discursive structure by proposing an amendment on the issue. When the conversation focused on the wording of the amendment and the difficulty of its implementation due to an "interpretive problem," she ultimately disclosed, "Look, when I submitted it, I just needed a space to voice this thought. I didn't mean for it to be an amendment necessarily, but I needed a space to have this discussion." In both elections, appeals were made to consider alternative perspectives on the issue, perspectives that were not necessarily antithetical to Islam and that would perhaps make visible other dimensions of religion (Islam). In both elections, however, a certain type of religion dominates the discourse: textual, legal, and, to some extent, paternalistic, not because Iman's and Ghada's amendments did not pass but because the *manner* in which they were engaged was inadequate. To the credit of the BU MSA leadership in both instances, they made transparent the point that the issue of women and prayer was a community concern and warranted further discussion, but elections as a mode of engaging them was not productive.

What does this mean for other Muslim students? Students like Amani took such exchanges to mean that the MSA discursive structures did not offer a platform where they could voice or engage their own religious views, which were more nuanced. For example, Amani's and Zara's perspective on female-led prayer made room for not just textual and juristic authority but also lived religion: while they were unsure of the prayer's juristic validity and were hesitant to attend themselves, they still thought it was important to keep it in place for others who attached themselves to an Islamic practice in a different way. Even Yusuf, who wasn't directly impacted by whether or not the practice stayed in place, was sensitive to the role of productive discourse in addressing the issue and to the failure of the existing discursive configuration in doing so. Attempts at reconfiguring the debate also failed, and from the resulting interactions students like Amani learned to keep private their religious beliefs and questions, even within a Muslim setting on campus.

Conclusion: What Religious Privatization Reveals

Thus far I have described what happens during the privatization process and explained why students privatize. When Muslim students at BU *do* encounter religion in campus discourse, the structure of that discourse reproduces specific notions of religion that limit their choices. On one hand, they encounter a liberal discourse that operates on assumptions that religion is private and subjective. On the other hand, they encounter a conservative discourse—in some ways a response to institutional secularity—that operates on assumptions that religion is textual and literal. Both of these choices are a result of a discursive structure configured by Protestant–secular logics; they point to the failure of categories vis-à-vis politics and religion, and ultimately they have the same outcome: they lead students to privatize their own religious ideas and beliefs.

To summarize, the Islamic Studies event on gender and the MSA elections represent opposite ends of the liberal/conservative rhetorical structure described by Jakobsen and Pellegrini.[38] Such a structure, as we can recall, limits the choices available to the liberal advocate of religion who wishes to engage religion in the public sphere while also engaging liberal values. Amani is a classic example of a liberal advocate of religion because she did not like her left/right choices on campus. As she noted, she *wanted* to discuss gender, race, and sexuality in relation to religion, but she found it difficult to do so both in Muslim settings and on campus generally. So, she opted to keep her views private.

So, what do these two case studies demonstrate? First, we learn how even when "religion is no longer invisible" on campus,[39] such as in settings I have described, the visibility of religion is partial. The version of religion that is *allowed to be* visible has to align within the discursive structures rooted in Protestant–secular logics, namely, the liberal/conservative binary. I should point out that while the academic event is institutionally organized and moderated, the MSA elections occur completely under the students' purview. It is important to consider them, however, because they represent a substructure within the institution in which Muslim students participate. Moreover, the tenor and nature of the substructure are often a reaction to institutional climate and context, as Binder and Wood have shown in their study on conservative college students.[40]Their investigation addresses political leanings and discourse, but their findings are generative in thinking about religious minorities on campus. In particular, they find that when a liberal college culture permeates their campus, conservative students tend to self-silence their political perspectives among peers and faculty, as well as in classrooms and coursework. Binder and Wood illustrate how this self-silence becomes a contributing factor in the development of conservative subcultures (in the form of clubs, for example) as a means of engaging their political views in terms of both discourse and activism.

Let me reiterate that while the MSA at BU does not represent the "religious right" per se, it *is* a substructure at BU, and, like many MSAs at a given time, it can be sometimes composed of "conservative gatekeepers [who are] struggling with hegemonic liberal secularity in the Muslim and campus communities as they construct representation and organize spaces."[41] Moreover, the MSA also represents a discursive space in which Muslim students seek to engage their religious beliefs, identities, and questions through various activities.[42] I describe the BU MSA elections, then, to illustrate how the discourse at this event (leaning conservative) is in contrast to the discourse at the Islamic Studies event (leaning liberal). These are the two choices available to students like Amani, who might not see their ideas meshing easily in either context and thus end up privatizing their views.

Second, these two case studies show that these limited choices also convey the inadequacy of labels and binaries vis-à-vis Muslims. Zareena Grewal, in her investigation of young American Muslims and their knowledge-seeking journeys, has shown that "the application of political categories such as 'liberal, 'progressive,' and 'conservative' fails to capture the varied perspectives and religious orientations of Muslim Americans."[43] The Islamic Studies event was too liberal and the MSA elections too conservative for students like Amani, who saw themselves more appropriately somewhere in the middle, but for whom the middle did not exist on campus.

Finally, these students' experiences and ideas about religion shed light on what I believe is an important point about the relationship between Islam and Protestantism: Islam is (obviously) not Protestantism, but more importantly, *Islam is also not the opposite of Protestantism.* Undoubtedly, Protestant features dominate the conventional understanding of religion: private, voluntary, individual, textual, and believed. Meanwhile, other religions, including Islam, are expected to have the *exact opposite* features: public, coercive, communal, oral, and enacted.[44] The problem with such a construction, however, is that—as the students' experiences reveal—Islam can have any combination of or all of these features for different people at different times. The dissonance that students like Amani experience at both types of events I described is that the "religion" visible at both events insufficiently captures *their* ideas about religion (Islam). For instance, at the Islamic Studies event, the "religion" visible is not textual enough; at the MSA elections, it is not lived enough. The events present them with an either/or option, whereas they believe it can be both/and.

What the religious privatization process ultimately reveals, then, is how the logics of a Protestant/secular framework make legible two opposing positions for Muslims students. There is nothing inherently problematic about the positions themselves, and the version of religion they make evident might very well work for some students (like Haaris, for example). However, reifying *only* two positions leaves out several other students who might otherwise be more comfortable with a third position (or fourth, or fifth, and so on). For them, the only option then is to keep their ideas of religion private and then attempt to engage them again in a different setting. However, for these students, privatization is still not the "end of the story," and they do take other steps to engage Islam and curate their lived Muslim experience on campus. This process is one of personalization, which I turn to next in the following chapter.

4

Personalization of Faith: Outside the "Protestant–Secular" Box

In prior chapters, we've seen how Muslim students at BU encounter religious pluralism and forms of religious discourses on campus in a context that is Protestant–secular. We began with a broad institutional context to illustrate how the university selectively accommodates and celebrates the diversity of Muslim students, amplifying their difference in the name of pluralism, which ultimately serves the goal of promoting its image as a secular and inclusive institution. Then, we moved to a narrower intracommunity context to show how the liberal/conservative rhetorical structure created by Protestant–secular logics is reproduced on campus, limiting the discursive choices for these Muslim students on campus in spaces that have been designated for discourse on Islam and Muslims.

From this analysis, it is evident that these students are in an "institutional container" that mitigates their Muslimness in ways that do not always work for them. Their story does not end here, however. In this final chapter, I narrow the scope further to the micro level, exploring the lived experiences of individual Muslim students to better understand how they negotiate Islam and their religious commitments. In doing so, I highlight the ways in which these students engage Islam and their Muslimness on their own terms; despite being embedded in an institution whose Protestant–secular context limits the set of possibilities available to them. At events such as the ones I described in the previous chapter, the only way out for these students is the way in, namely, to privatize their

Being Muslim on Campus. Abiya Ahmed, Oxford University Press. © Oxford University Press 2026.
DOI: 10.1093/9780197773628.003.0005

ideas and beliefs. While that approach suffices for them in the moment, the issue of limited possibilities is one that they encounter even otherwise on campus because the institution and institutional substructures consistently put their religion in a box. So, what do they do? How do they go about being Muslim on campus?

Through the individual cases of three students, I show that they engage and, in some ways, resist the Protestant–secular ideological apparatus of the institution via a process of personalizing their engagement with Islam and Muslimness. I define personalization as **a strategy by which these students thoughtfully apply agency and autonomy to engage Islam and be Muslim on campus in ways that make sense for them.** Personalization is a necessary strategy that these students develop specifically within the context of a Protestant–secular institution "container" that wants to contain their religion and expressions of religiosity, where the dominant Protestant–secular framework is one in which they do not quite fit. In this sense, personalization is a story about these students' agency and autonomy.

In another sense, personalization is also a story about religious change (or lack of it) on campus. What happens to emerging adults' religious commitments when they enter a new environment and stage of their lives? We do not know much about what this process of religious change looks like for Muslim students in secular settings, particularly at a campus where Protestant–secularity, sometimes formally and other times informally, dictates the terms of engagement with Islam and Muslimness. Do these Muslim students change their religious beliefs and commitments? If so, what does this change look like? Is it a compromise on or giving up of these commitments in the face of external factors, or is it a turn inward and staunch protection of these commitments? Much of the research on the relationship between students' religious change and college makes the case that students individualize their religious beliefs and commitments in college.[1] However, I propose that religious individualism does not fully capture the range and nuances of these students' agency and autonomy, and we can better understand Muslim students' religious change in college as personalization, versus characterizing their change as individualism or even just privatization.

Why should this distinction be made? Because personalization is different from both privatization and individualism in important ways. Privatization is only an *element* of personalization and fails to account for other moves that students make throughout their college experience. Meanwhile, individualism is typically understood *as* privatization and elevation of internal authority.[2] When disaggregated, however, individualism yields important other features such as agency, autonomy, and distance from authority.[3] Insofar as these Muslim students' personalization is also an exercise in agency and autonomy, it could be considered individualism. However, it is not absolute individualism because even as the students make a move away from some external authorities toward internal choices, they also acknowledge *other* external authorities. Moreover, the faith engagement process of these students is not an isolated one, as typically it also includes an element of community. Because individualism and privatization fail to account for both of these nuances, I find that personalization is broader than both and better encompasses the totality of the students' experience.

Religious Individualism and College Students

Much has been written about the effect of the college experience on students' religious beliefs and commitments. Originally, it was held that college led students to abandon their faith—a conclusion that has since been questioned by both quantitative and qualitative studies.[4] Recent research has shifted the terms of the debate, as Mayrl and Oeur note: "the question is now less about whether students' religious commitments are maintained or abandoned, and more about whether they are ignored or reconstituted during the college years."[5] Thus, there has been a move to understand what exactly happens to students' religious commitments and beliefs in college—or, in other words, what *kind* of religious change occurs.

This question of religious change, in turn, has been answered in two ways. One set of research shows that college has a significant impact on students' spiritual and religious beliefs, as shown most comprehensively by Astin, Astin, and Lindholm in their landmark study *Cultivating the Spirit.*[6] More specifically for our purposes, those who build on the claim that college has an impact point also to the trend of individualization. For example, in their review of religion and higher education, Mayrl and Oeur note that college students' interest in religion and spirituality is broad and not deep. They write that "the more time and investment religion requires of them, the less likely students are to engage," and thus while they might believe in God and occasionally pray, they are less likely to be members of campus organizations or to attend services.[7] In other words, this aligns with the typical idea of individualism as a move away from community and institutional commitment to what suits the self at a given stage in one's life. Similarly, in their qualitative study of four campuses, Cherry, DeBerg, and Porterfield also determine that the college experience reduces religious orthodoxy and leads to more individualistic commitments.[8] Recent research by Flory and Denton on emerging adults—a category within which college students fall—also points to the conclusion that they are turning away from formal religious beliefs, practices, and participation in religious institutions.[9]

At the same time, another body of research makes the almost opposite claim that college has minimal impact on students' religious beliefs. In this camp, a common reference is Tim Clydesdale's "identity lockbox" theory, in which he concludes that students stow away their religious identities in a "lockbox" during their college years because they are too busy with other demands of being in college, and they return to these identities and commitments years later when they graduate.[10] Mayrl and Uecker, too, arrived at similar findings when comparing college students and nonstudents to isolate the impact of college on several dependent variables, including religious individualism and religious independence. Their findings indicate that college attendance is not significantly correlated with either and that social networks, service attendance, and parental relationships are far more closely related to religious individualism and independence.[11]

Essentially then, we have the possibility that students will either enter college and undergo a process of religious change that will inevitably also change their commitment to original beliefs and attachment to community; or that they will not really engage with their beliefs and commitments for the duration of their college career, setting them aside and safeguarding them, which will preserve for them these commitments to which they will return once they complete college.

In this chapter, I show that for the Muslim students I spent time with, both of these perspectives hold: the religious change these Muslim students undergo is one in which they individualize their faith engagement to some extent, but that engagement is a strategy they adopt to keep their beliefs intact. In other words, *some change happens, but that change occurs in the service of preserving beliefs.* This process is a highly agentic and autonomous one that simultaneously acknowledges a need for some kind of authority and/or community even as it makes a move away from other kinds. This process, I argue, is one of personalization, and viewing it as such helps us understand religious change in a different way.

My rendering of personalization aligns with Adhami's recent work on detailing American Muslim journeys of "personal authenticity" and its intersection with piety. Adhami carefully documents the engagement of Boston Muslims with Islam and Muslimness, their crises of faith, and their doubts, ultimately showing us that their lived Islam, even as it sometimes hinges on doctrinal authority, is less about perfect certainty and more about having consistent commitment and fidelity to the tradition and to the community.[12] BU Muslim students, even as they undergo some changes in how they view or engage their Islam and Muslimness, stay connected to the tradition and/or community.

Finally, exploring the case of Muslim students to interrogate dominant perspectives on religious change in college is also worthwhile because the trends they do exhibit—that we know of—tend to be against the grain. Astin, Astin, and Lindholm found that compared to other religious groups, Muslim students are highly likely to be on a spiritual quest and least likely to be skeptical about their faith. In addition, Astin et al. highlight that of all the religions and denominations they researched, Muslim students are the only group that "show an increase in frequent attendance at religious services during college."[13] These trends point to something other than the "change" versus "no-change" framing because a spiritual quest could indicate an element of engaging one's beliefs, whereas lack of skepticism and an increase in attendance could indicate not only a need for community but also an attempt to stay attached to one's faith. Relatedly, as Small has discussed in her work on faith frames, not all students experience religiosity and spirituality in the same way. Thus, what religious change looks like for Muslim students could be different from what it looks like for others.[14]

As a minority religio-racial group in college, Muslim students offer an interesting case study that can be used to investigate the dominant narratives of religious change on campus. For this interrogation, I delve deeper into individualism to understand how it applies to Muslim students. Thus, their case also helps deconstruct religious individualism in general. Before we get to the students, then, exploring the concept of religious individualism in more depth will provide helpful context.

Disaggregated Religious Individualism

To frame the personalization process, I start with the concept of individualism but, instead of leveraging it as a whole, I defer to its disaggregated form.[15] When disaggregated, other features of individualism become apparent, with agency and autonomy being key. Moreover, as we will see in the case of three Muslim students, agency and autonomy are not disconnected from religious authority and ideas about normativity. All of these concepts help clarify the personalization process that BU Muslim students make during college and what that means for the kind of religious change that occurs.

Let's start, however, with religious individualism and perhaps most appropriately with *Habits of the Heart*, in which Robert Bellah and his colleagues examine American individualism within various spheres, including religion.[16] In particular, religious individualism has come to be strongly associated with "Sheilaism"—named after Sheila Larson, a nurse interviewed by Bellah et al., who describes her personal faith as being grounded in her "own little voice," which instructs her primarily to be good to oneself and others. Bellah et al. consider Sheilaism to be representative of a private, individual faith that privileges personal experience and "is rooted in the effort to transform external authority into internal meaning.[17]" Since its first appearance in 1986, "Sheilaism"—as a proxy for individualized or privatized religion—has been quite generative and the subject of much reflection and research within various contexts.[18]

Religious individualism, of course, can also be understood more broadly as a feature of American individualism: having "loose organizational connections" and "porous institutions,"[19] ultimately leading people to turn away from community and social organization.[20] Elsewhere, Bellah discusses in depth the theological roots of such individualism, noting how it is a "deep cultural code" embedded in American society, which has its roots in Protestantism.[21] Similarly, Porterfield has pointed out that privileging internal experience as a source of religious authority and affording it transcendent value began as a Protestant phenomenon with the Puritans. Later, it was also embodied in the lives and works of Transcendentalists such as Henry David Thoreau and

Ralph Waldo Emerson, who we today consider champions of individualism writ large.[22]

Within this discourse, John O'Brien's intervention calls into question dominant constructions of individualism by way of disaggregating it.[23] In his study of religious Americans, O'Brien points out that typical formulations of American individualism are built on the works of scholars like Bellah, Wuthnow, and Putnam, whose conclusions are based on studies of "middle-class, mostly white Americans and therefore focus exclusively on the three elements of individualism's cultural content most evident among those parties: voluntarism (considering action as an individual choice), self-actualization (prioritizing development of the self), and privatization (moving away from social commitment and organization)." Building on multiple other treatments of individualism and its related meanings, O'Brien adds to this list "autonomy (freedom from social influence), reflexivity (stepping back to reflect on one's social position), and agency (making individual effort)."[24] In my analysis, agency and autonomy emerge as the tools with which Muslim students personalize their lived experience and thus attempt to inhabit a Muslimness that does not fit in the Protestant–secular institutional box. Unlike the white Americans who have been typically the subjects of research and have set the terms of individualism, Muslim students are religiously and racially marked subjects whose experiences cannot be understood in those terms alone. Rather, their "individualism" must necessarily have other dimensions.

In this regard, O'Brien also takes issue with imagining American individualism as a national "deep cultural code" as Bellah has done. According to O'Brien, such a notion implies that individualism's powerful history has inescapable imprints upon average people today, "directing social actors to talk and act in ways that reflect a limited range of individualistic meanings." Instead, O'Brien, leveraging Swidler,[25] aims to construe individualism as a "strategy of action" whereby

> Religious Americans creatively respond to the cultural dilemma of participating in communally demanding and externally authoritative religious lives within a culturally individualistic context by mobilizing meanings of autonomy and agency to project a self differentiated from religious authority and routine religious behavior.[26]

Let's break that down. Essentially, O'Brien's framework of individualism has (1) a socially structured dilemma and (2) a response to this dilemma. He contends that the dilemma has on one end institutionalized religion, or participation in normative practices, or deference to external authority (or all of the above); and, on the other, the overarching cultural expectation of individualism, demanding that the self and its needs and preferences take precedence over those of the community or tradition. O'Brien analyzes cases of religious Americans (from his own fieldwork and that of others) to conclude that the response to such a dilemma is the use of "individualism as a creative strategy of action." In this formulation, he argues, autonomy and agency take center stage. Religious Americans leverage autonomy to assert that their religious or spiritual belief is not tied to external authority or a hierarchy and agency to assert their own effort and volition in adhering to normative practices (as opposed to blindly following them). O'Brien's "rethinking characterizes individualism not as a single inherited tradition but as an internally varied strategy of action through which everyday Americans work to differentiate themselves from religious authority and routine religious behaviors."[27]

Religious authority is important here because secularization is often considered to be a decline not of religion per se but of religious authority,[28] and so much of individualism and its features have to do with where one places religious authority: within institutions, other people, texts, the self, or some combination of the above. Sheilaism is indicative of elevating individual experience to some level of "cosmic principle," and, as Porterfield has noted, the contention between Sheila and her critics is a matter of *degree*, namely, "the degree to which individual religious experience should be the arbiter of religious life and the degree to which individual religious experience is the source of religion's genuinely salutary effects."[29] In other words, if religious authority were to be placed on a continuum with internal on one end and external on the other, Sheilaism would fall on the extreme internal end of the pole. For this reason, O'Brien has noted that Sheilaism—while certainly associated with privatization—is also indicative of autonomy, or a "symbolic distance" from the influence of human religious authority.[30] In my analysis, I also discuss where BU Muslim students place religious authority and how they use autonomy and agency—features of a disaggregated individualism—in interacting with it.

Thus, O'Brien's reconceptualization and disaggregation of individualism help frame the lived experience of BU Muslim students because it allows us to conceive of personalization, too, as a strategy of action. This strategy (1) centers their agency and autonomy in a hegemonic context or institutional container that considers them as objects; and (2) allows them to remain tethered to some kind of religious authority, community, and tradition on their own terms. So, although I use O'Brien's disaggregation of individualism and apply his conception of it as a strategy of action, I also argue that the simultaneous application of agency and autonomy *while remaining attached to a preferred religious authority or community* implies that these students' strategy is something other than just individualism. For this reason, I find it more appropriate to characterize their strategy as personalization.

In what follows, I discuss three students: Idris, Amira, and Amani. Each student's case involves a dilemma[31] that is sometimes triggered by an event, a class, or broader discourses on an issue that may lead students to reveal their moral politics and beliefs about normativity. Situations or issues that lead to a consideration of moral politics offer a robust site for analyzing issues of individualism because religious individualism is often correlated with moral progressivism when assuming that religious authority is placed squarely with the individual.[32] Students respond to these dilemmas both discursively in conversation with me and in other actions they take during their college experience. While each student responds in unique, personalized ways, illustrating varying levels and forms of autonomy and agency, each of them also reveals some consistency about where religious authority lies.

Idris

In 2018, the Friday before Thanksgiving break, Idris and I were chatting over *halal* burgers from a campus eatery. We were seated across from each other in an empty conference room on the second floor of the student center. The last time we had had an in-depth conversation was about a month before, though I had seen him on and off at events and in passing. He had been busy, he told me, because he was reading the Qur'an for the first time in English.

Which translation was it, I asked? He put his burger down and said, "I'll show you." He started rummaging through his backpack, then looked up, "Wait, is it okay if I show you?" "Of course," I replied. In the next few seconds, he pulled out his copy. It was Abdullah Yusuf Ali's translation, one of the more common ones. "This was my dad's," he told me.

"How's the reading going?" I asked.

"It's going well. I have the bad habit of starting books and then not finishing them, but this is one of the times I've kept going. I even read it while walking!"

I asked him if he was reading on his own or as part of a group. "On my own," he replied as he wolfed down his waffle fries. After a sip of his Mountain Dew, he added, "I haven't found anyone that I think would be able to help me with that, particularly here at school."

We discussed the lack of Islamic Studies classes on campus where he could potentially find space for discourse. Then I asked, "What about MSA events?"

"I'm on their mailing list, but I don't go very much to their events."

"And MCC events?"

"Those I'm particularly hesitant about," he said without a beat. The conviction with which he said that more than piqued my curiosity, so I asked him to elaborate.

"Certain times I find that when people there [at MCC] speak about Islam, they're not speaking about Islam. They're mostly speaking about social justice and leftism, and I'm not there for that. I'm there to learn about my religion. If I wanna have a political conversation with you, I can, but I don't want to be there for that when I'm looking for something on religion. If I'm there for religion, then I wanna be there for *that*," he explained.

I asked him how he had arrived at the conclusion that MCC events were more about politics than religion. "I went to that one event with, what's her name . . . Zaynab," he said. I thought he might be referring to the event on gender, but he said, "it was only last week, the one about her thing in the South."

Idris was referring to a different event, which was part of a series of talks organized and hosted by the MCC (unlike the gender event, which the Islamic Studies program had organized for which MCC had just offered its space). This one featured Zaynab, the BU Muslim chaplain, and her experiences in the "Bible Belt," as she termed it. Between Donald Trump's 2016 election and inauguration, she had taken a road trip through various Southern states, so the MCC had invited her as a guest speaker to share her experiences. I had attended and noticed other Muslim students there, though I must have missed seeing Idris. He was there though, as he noted, and had serious misgivings about Zaynab's perspectives.

Zaynab had shared that while she traveled widely and met several people along the way, "two recurring themes stand out: salvation and abortion." The people she met during her journey—such as a Mormon man on a bus ride from Salt Lake City to Mississippi, or a Southern Baptist woman in a small Texan village—were strongly anti-abortion and delighted that Donald Trump had vowed "to ban abortion in every state." In her narrative, Zaynab did not explicitly say she was pro-choice, but she did recount instances of trying to offer that perspective to her interlocuters, reasoning that women should have the right to choose regardless but, as a bare minimum, be allowed that choice in case of extenuating circumstances.

Idris thought Zaynab's story was interesting but that her views were "weird." He singled out abortion in particular. What was he expecting, I asked? "I expected her to inject her religion a lot more into the story, considering that she's Muslim, but it was more focused on political ideology." Idris said he thought "Islamically abortion is not okay, except when the mother's life is in jeopardy but, besides that, no." He wondered why Zaynab hadn't said that—both to those she met on her trip and at the MCC talk. "That's what I mean by not talking about Islam, just talking about all this leftist stuff."

During my fieldwork, I conducted six formal interviews with Idris, in addition to chatting with him informally and observing him several times. Abortion came up often in our conversations, either because it was the direct subject of discussion (as in Zaynab's event) or as an example of Muslims engaging in "leftist" politics. Once I asked him how he arrived at the conclusion that "Islamically abortion is not okay." He replied, "God thinks life is valuable. He gave it to us. Why should the most innocent among us should have their lives taken?" And so, he was bothered that Zaynab had omitted what he considered the "Islamic" perspective on abortion: "I don't see any justification according to the Qur'an to kill your baby." Another time we were discussing Hamza Yusuf, a popular American Muslim academic and public intellectual, whom Idris admired and whose videos he would watch from time to time on YouTube. In that particular conversation, I had asked

Idris where he thought Hamza Yusuf might fall on the political spectrum. "Probably center left but a lot more nuanced than other people. He'd probably say abortion is not okay," Idris replied.

I mention these conversations and abortion in particular because it gives us important information about Idris: first, it illustrates his moral politics, with abortion as a case of that. For Idris, his moral politics are aligned with his religious beliefs, which he considers to be normative. In this sense, his dilemma is slightly different from O'Brien's "socially structured dilemma," which has institutionalized religion, normativity, and external authority on one end and individualism on the other.[33] In contrast, Idris's predicament is that, for him, instead of normativity being situated with "institutionalized religion on campus," he feels that *he* is the one being normatively Islamic when it comes to issues like abortion, and that the external religious authority on campus (Zaynab) and the organized Muslim community (MSA, MCC) actually does not represent normative Islam. Second, it helps us distill where he places religious authority. Note how he substantiates his own view on abortion and dismisses Zaynab's: he attributes them to God and the Qur'an when he says "God thinks life is valuable" and "I don't see any justification according to the Qur'an to kill your baby." In other words, he places some authority with God and in the Qur'an. This was also evident in other conversations we had, in which he mentioned he was not convinced about the authenticity and authority of the Hadith tradition, but that he believed in God and the divinity of the Qur'an. As is evident in the description above, he was excited about reading the Qur'an in English and extrapolating from it what he considered Islamic views. He believed he was going through this process independently: "for me, religion is about text, and in Muslim community spaces on campus, I didn't feel like they had a focus on the text or what God wanted us to do, so it's mostly just been me trying to learn by myself, reading and formulating." Thus, in the sense that Idris was not part of some sort of Qur'an circle or learning its exegetical meanings with a scholar or academic, it was an independent process.

However, he said he *had* tried to meet Zaynab to discuss Islam and Islamic issues, but he had been unsuccessful in scheduling. After the MCC event where he heard Zaynab discuss her travels, he did not try again because he felt her approach to religion was colored by liberal politics. Meanwhile, he was able to talk to a Lutheran pastor on campus because he was more accessible, and Idris felt he could discuss his own faith easily with him. In addition, he was also active for a while in the College Republicans, Young America Foundation, and Turning Point USA on campus——all politically conservative entities. During his participation, he met and became close with conservative Christians, and, as he told me once, "The Muslim friends I do have, we don't really talk about religion. I speak more so to Christians about religion, than Muslims."

Idris's Personalization

What does all of this mean for Idris's personalization process on campus? Recall that personalization is a strategy through which students thoughtfully exercise agency and autonomy in order to engage Islam and be Muslim on campus. In Idris's case, his agency is evident in his individual effort to read and understand the Qur'an, as well as his move toward what he considers normativity. Saba Mahmood has shown convincingly that while agency is typically imagined as an exercise in resisting normativity, *moves that reinforce normativity can also be agentic.*[34] O'Brien also acknowledges this point when he notes that "actors can exercise their own agency—or effort—in the direction of and keeping with normative social, cultural, or religious expectations and not necessarily in opposition to them."[35] Thus, Idris's personalization process, in part, is a move away from the campus Muslim authority and community and toward what he considers normativity. His agency is thus an exercise by which he preserves his moral politics and religious beliefs (which, for him, are aligned).

In addition, O'Brien's autonomy is evident in his attempt to distance himself from Zaynab and what he considered to be the perspectives of the campus Muslim community. O'Brien defines autonomy as "distance from the influence of human religious authority,"[36] and he shows how the religious Americans in his study discursively distance themselves from external religious authorities to express their own selves as independent. They do this by emphasizing a personal and direct relationship with God or by disassociating from institutionalized or organized religion. Idris also did both but with a twist. He distanced himself from Zaynab as an external religious authority, and, given her position as the campus Muslim chaplain, he perceived her to be representative of the entire BU Muslim community and its approach to religion. He therefore also distanced himself from the organized campus Muslim community, while continuing to have a personal relationship with the Qur'an and God. The twist, of course, is that he still sought *some* community and authority, which he sometimes found in other religious figures such as Hamza Yusuf or a pastor on campus or in other students more aligned with his conservative political/sociocultural views.

In sum, Idris's personalization strategy allowed him to exercise agency and autonomy to change his alignments with authority and community in order to preserve his beliefs. His spiritual quest[37] led him to turn away from the campus Muslim authority (Zaynab) and Muslim community, and so his attendance at Muslim religious services on campus actually did decrease. For Idris, BU's institutional substructures designated for Islam and Muslims were colored by "leftist politics," and he thought the Muslims on campus had succumbed to that agenda, so he distanced himself from them. However, he did attach himself to other forms of authority (the Qur'an, God) and campus resources (the pastor, Christian friends), indicating that his engagement with his beliefs was not absolute individualism. Rather, his religious engagement in college was personalized in ways that allowed him to keep his beliefs while changing his external alignments.

Amira

If we compare Idris's case to Amira's, we again see the enactment of agency and autonomy but in a different direction: Amira moved away from what she considered normativity. Idris did not spend enough time with the campus Muslim community to explore the various dimensions and shades of its diversity. Had he done so, he might have discovered that the perspectives and approach of the Muslim Student Association (MSA) very much paralleled his own. But Amira did spend a lot of time with the campus Muslim community. When I first met her, she was part of the social justice team in the MSA and was interning at the MCC. She had mentioned to me then she was excited to contribute to the BU Muslim experience. I was in the participant observation stage at the time, and a few months later after I had selected her as a more in-depth case study for my project, we decided to schedule a formal interview.

By the time we were ready to conduct a formal interview, Amira had left the MSA social justice team. "What happened?" I asked. She replied, "I just wasn't getting what I thought I would get out of it. I wasn't enjoying it. There seemed to be a hesitation to new ideas or a desire to edge on the safe side of things." When I asked her to elaborate, she explained that she had tried to pitch ideas about "gender justice, for example" and they were met with resistance. "Originally, I thought I could stick it out and test the boundaries, but I just wasn't into that anymore. And I found that I could do the kinds of events and implement ideas that I wanted at the MCC, so I thought I might as well focus on my energies there."

As I continued to spend time with Amira throughout her sophomore and junior years, I saw that she did, in fact, focus her energies very much on programming at the MCC. She had been the one who had organized the talk with Zaynab that Idris had attended. In contrast to Idris's views on it, Amira thought the talk and its content was "really great." Her opinion of Zaynab in general was positive, and she considered her a legitimate Muslim authority: "I trust her with asking her questions about confusions about religion or just life in general," she told me once. With reference to the talk, I asked Amira what she thought of Zaynab's views on abortion. "Very similar to mine," she responded, "pro-choice under any circumstances." She also agreed with Zaynab's views on salvation: "Look, as long as you're a good person, right? Like I think all religions at the core of them are like good character, morals, that kind of thing, so being one religion over another I don't think is any kind of impediment."

As part of her work with the MCC, Amira had also once organized a Queer Muslim *iftar* (fast-breaking meal) that I had attended. According to her, "these issues are pushed under the rug, and we need to highlight them." By "these" she meant issues of queerness within the Muslim community, and her goal with the *iftar* event was to center queer Muslim voices as well as offer them a community experience in Ramadan. The iftar included a panel of queer Muslim students who narrated their experiences, struggles, and hopes. It was well attended by various students, including some Muslim students and Zaynab.

A couple of days after the event, I asked Amira how she felt about it. She was pleased: "It went very well I thought. I didn't expect to see many Muslims from the MSA there anyway, but overall, it was good to see some Muslim students attend, as well as others. And I really appreciated how the speakers were able to be so vulnerable and hopeful at the same time." Why did she think the issue was pushed under the rug, I asked? She replied, "Well, there's the story of Lot in the Qur'an and the entire city was destroyed because of homosexual activity. Based off that story, it's just a no-no essentially."

"So how would you respond to someone if they said, 'Well if that's the case, why are you supporting queer folks?'" I countered.

She nodded, paused for a bit, and then responded, "Yeah. I think the way I see it, Allah made you the way you are and He doesn't make mistakes. So, if you are gay, that's what you are and clearly, it's not something that you easily choose to do, considering there's so much backlash to it. If that's how you are, then you have every right to be accepted and to live in this society as a normal person." A little later in that conversation we were discussing her political orientations, and I asked her if she sometimes found her religion at odds with her political views. "Yes, but I've always maybe even looked for a way to reconcile the two and openly and actively embraced whatever reason I can find to reconcile the two. I don't know how proper that is, and sometimes I do feel guilty about testing the boundaries."

"Can you think of an example?" I asked.

"Kind of like the chains of logic that I just went through. So, with gay rights, Allah made you this way and this kind of logic, or the same with abortion—the idea of a choice," she explained.

Amira's views on abortion, queerness, and salvation are relevant for two reasons: first, they reveal her liberal/progressive orientation and moral politics on these issues; and second, they indicate where she places religious authority: with herself, God, the Qur'an, and figures like Zaynab whose perspectives align with hers.

Amira, like Idris, strongly emphasized the authority of the Qur'an, and she saw it and Islam as a source of morality. Asked about Islamic practice once, she said: "I try to practice. I try to read the Qur'an, to pray. I've grown up very much with the Qur'an and with the lessons of the Qur'an, and I see Islam as morality in a sense and I really like the traits and the character that Islam tries to instill. I also am very in tune with the community aspect of it as well because I basically practically grew up in the *masjid* [mosque], so community is important to me."

Amira's Personalization

Amira's personalization process is both similar to and different from Idris's. It is similar in the sense that she also changed her external alignments to preserve her moral politics and religious beliefs. It is different because unlike Idris, who moved away from the campus Muslim context altogether, Amira moved from one Muslim context to another—from what she considered a normative Muslim context to one that aligns with her moral politics. In that sense, she is also different from Idris because he believed his moral politics to be aligned with his religious beliefs. Meanwhile, Amira struggled a little to reconcile her moral politics with her religious beliefs, but she was able to alleviate that struggle somewhat once she moved from one context to another.

For Amira then, agency and autonomy became evident in her choice to leave the MSA and distance herself from that particular version of institutionalized religion. In O'Brien's analysis, the subjects are concerned with differentiating themselves from religious authority and normative behaviors.[38] Amira did that too. Unlike Idris, she found normativity with the campus Muslim community at the MSA, and she made a move away from it. Like Idris, however, she did not completely detach herself from authority and community. Whereas Idris found it outside of the institutional Muslim context altogether, Amira found it in a different Muslim context on campus. Because engagement with her faith and community remained important to her, she focused on the MCC, which allowed her to channel her perspectives into the events and activities she deemed important to her Muslim experience. Her comments on the "chains of logic" to reconcile her perspectives also indicate that she attempted to reconcile her own moral politics with her ideas about what is Islamic, which she derived from the Qur'an. Even in that reconciliation, however, she acknowledged the authority of God ("Allah made you this way, and He doesn't make mistakes"). Vogel and Bellah have noted that mainline

Protestant Christianity has a strong sense of moral judgment and a low tolerance for inconsistency.[39] In Amira's case, however, we do in fact see a strong sense of moral judgment but a *high* tolerance for inconsistency. Even if her reconciliation efforts fall short of being completely satisfactory to her at times (as she said, she did not know "how proper" her "chains of logic," were and she did "feel guilty about testing boundaries"), the inconsistencies did not stop her from being Muslim in ways that made sense to her and from engaging with Islam.

Inasmuch as her choices reflect a level of agency and autonomy, her experience indicates what kind of religious change she undergoes as she curates her lived Muslim experience on campus. Moreover, her personalization strategy is that to some extent she defies the liberal/conservative binary by taking a liberal approach to controversial issues while also attaching herself to community, scripture, and external authority.

Amani

We turn next to Amani, whom we have seen already in various community contexts such as the gender event and the MSA elections. In this chapter, I bring in a specific classroom context to illustrate her autonomy and agency in personalizing her Muslim experience on campus. Amani's dilemma here is unlike Idris's and Amira's. She does not struggle with community here as her dilemma's context is actually not a Muslim one; but it is nevertheless a macro institutional context that offers insight into her own agency and autonomy in personalizing her faith.

The class themes were decolonization, Black feminism explored through the lens of spirituality, performance, ritual, and magic. Amani had mentioned the course during an earlier interview, and I had emailed the instructor to ask if I could attend. The instructor politely declined permission "due to the depth of the spiritual and investigative process" but invited me to attend an upcoming public session with a guest speaker. I accepted.

And so, I arrived at the campus aerobics center and gym, where the class was usually held. While I waited, I recalled my initial conversation with Amani a couple of weeks before when she had mentioned the class. Her mom was "freaking out," she had told me, because she was taking a "dance and magic" class. Amani's instructor was a Yoruba priest who believed in orishas and deities. "Of course, I don't believe that," she had said, "coz that's *shirk*,[40] IMO. No, not IMO, it IS *shirk*! But I told her [the instructor] that I fundamentally don't believe in this, and she was very understanding. She told me, 'Yeah, no worries. If it resonates with you, do that. If it doesn't, don't.' So she's chill."

At the gym, I couldn't see Amani around in the class just yet. There was a sign-up sheet for visitors, and we had to take our shoes and backpacks off to leave them in the corner. I did that and joined the circle that was already forming in the middle of the room. There were about fifteen people so far—I was not sure how many visitors and how many actual students. The instructor was helping the guest speaker get organized.

In a few minutes, Amani introduced him as Gary J. Smith,[41] a poet, writer, and public theologian, among other things. Shortly after, he introduced himself and his history as a Black gay poet, performer, and later an ordained minister. "And now I'm trying to bring it all together—the creative, the poetic, the prophetic . . . and I insist on bringing all these things to every space—that I inhabit." He spoke slowly and carefully, and when he was finished introducing himself, he took out a candle and said, "What I'd like to do is . . . I rarely do this in public . . . umm . . . ," he said, as he clicked a lighter and lit the candle, "but . . . umm . . . and I understand that there were many different faiths and no faiths traditions umm . . . and . . . ," he paused, as he clicked the lighter again and lit another candle, and then continued, "so participate as witness, put your invisible shield up if you don't want none of this. It's alright . . . it is not . . . I would never bring anything to harm . . . umm . . . my whole life and work is about getting us free, and I want us all to get free from . . . whatever."

Both candles were now lit, and he was ready to begin. I looked around and noticed that Amani had come in and was already part of the circle. "So, this was my New Year's prayer that my cousin in New Orleans sent to me, and said I needed to say over my whole house. And since y'all are in my house right now, imma say it over you all . . ." He began the prayer, moving slowly around the circle, using his hand to push away the smoke from the candle's flame, beginning each sentence in his prayer with "I break and release myself from all curses . . ." and ending it with ". . . . in the name of Jesus." As he moved around the circle, I glanced at Amani, who was facing downward with her eyes closed.

When Gary finished, he explained the ceremony he was about to conduct, which paid tribute to African American traditions, ancestors, and women. The rest of the class included breathing exercises, recitation of poetry penned by Black women, and a short writing task we all did to honor women who had played a special role in our lives. The class ended with Smith emphasizing the power of "calling on our ancestral women when fighting forces of patriarchy and capitalism."

Amani had to rush to another class, and so I wasn't able to debrief with her right then, but a week later during our late Friday afternoon conversation at the student center, I asked about her thoughts on the session that Gary led. She responded, "Oh yeah, I liked the idea of taking down the patriarchy and capitalism. I mean this class is all about breaking barriers and decolonizing." Then she paused and added, "I don't know how I felt about the whole Jesus stuff though."

"Say more," I urged.

"Well, I am clear about drawing lines in this class, and I know what my intentions are. And Gary, he had said we were free to create 'an invisible shield' if we didn't want to be a part of his prayer. So that's what I did, 'cause like I said, it borders on *shirk* sometimes, and . . . I mean I ain't praying to Jesus!" she explained, and then continued: "It taught me a lot, this class, it did. Some things I took, some things I didn't. Some things I engaged in, some things I did not. But I took the feminism discourse, the decolonial theory—I took all of that."

There is much to say about this course, but an important preface is that at a campus that foregrounds scientific and secular pursuits, this class was not necessarily teaching about religion but integrating some form of religion and spirituality into its subject matter. Thus, two separate religious alignments have been made evident to Amani. The first is her awareness of her instructor's beliefs in orishas and deities; and the second is Gary's session where he brings in a Christian element and prayer to the decolonial Black feminism discourse. In both cases, the instructor and Gary integrate their own spiritual/religious perspectives into the course material. Such integration illustrates two things: first, it is indeed a feature of what Jacobsen and Jacobsen call the "pluriform" era of religion and higher education, where religion is not only more visible but also more diverse. Its full engagement especially in this course is a nod toward "rejection of objective epistemology" whereby universities and colleges have "begun to emphasize the multifaceted nature of learning and the importance of epistemological diversity within the scholarly community."[42] Second, it is also an intervention into status quo in that the class instructor, a Black Yoruba priest, and Gary, a Black, gay, ordained minister are able to confidently integrate their religious/spiritual beliefs and praxis into a classroom at a secular university. As Shahjahan has shown, not much research has been done on how faculty of color let their spirituality inform their teaching practices, particularly in relation to social justice.[43] In Amani's class, we see how Gary does that in this session. Although I did not observe any of the other sessions (as they were private) and thus did not have first-hand experience with the instructor's pedagogy, I did hear about it from Amani. She told me that much of the class revolved around performance (dance in some form) and embodied practice to provoke social change, particularly around feminism.

However, even as Gary and the instructor make their religious/spiritual beliefs visible in the course by integrating them, Amani herself has to deal with the dilemma of reconciling her own Islamic beliefs with the overarching paradigm of the class. As she told me, "The class and its final project [which was a performance] was rooted very much in traditional African religions which are considered polytheistic. So, I was very worried about crossing the line especially regarding monotheism."

Amani's Personalization

So, then, what did Amani do? Before we answer that question, it is helpful to note that Amani was, by her own admission, a "feminist" who avidly followed not only popular Muslim women activists such as Linda Sarsour and Zahra Billoo, but also the work of Muslim women academics such as Amina Wadud and Asma Barlas. "I like them, I know people don't like them, but I like them," Amani told me once, about Wadud and Barlas. I inquired as to why she thought people did not like them.

This was her reply: "Because they're counter hegemonic and they threaten the people who have authority on the interpretations and the way that we practice Islam, all the way down to the nitty-gritty. But they resonate more with me. I haven't done enough research for me to be comfortable in asserting those positions myself, but they [Wadud and Barlas] sit well with me."

Amani's comments indicate her moral politics vis-à-vis feminism, as well as whom she considered authoritative in that regard: Muslim women figures whom she thought represented the consonance of her religious beliefs and moral politics as far as gender and feminism were concerned. This alignment is important because her dilemma in her class is not about reconciling her religious beliefs with her moral politics, as it was in Idris's and Amira's case. In Amani's case, the dilemma is about reconciling an epistemological framework that she believes to be definitionally un-Islamic (polytheism) with the value of the content being framed (feminism, liberation, gender justice, etc.) that, for her, could be Islamic.

What she did then, was personalize both her class experience and her engagement with Islam to suit her needs in ways that work for her. With respect to the class in general, she let the lead instructor know that she did not believe in orishas and deities, to which the instructor responded that she could do whatever resonated with her. Amani took this response to mean that she would "draw lines" in the class, and the lines would become sharper in Gary's ceremonial prayer to Jesus, which visibly unsettled her. However, instead of feeling boxed in by drawing those lines, Amani empowered herself by being autonomous and agentic in how she experienced the class. The first move she made, then, was one of autonomy: she distanced herself from the religious/spiritual authority of her instructor (and Gary) and reverted to her Islamic beliefs: "I think my biggest concern overall was with polytheism and the different spirits/orishas that were referenced. And so, the way I thought about it was that all of these creations (the ocean, fire, sun, moon) are reflections of Allah's Power and Beauty and that's where I came from. Sometimes I was worried that it was crossing principles of *tawheed* [monotheism] but the way I thought about it felt truthful and gave me time to reflect more about Allah and the universe and just be more grateful," she explained.

The second move was one of agency through which she exerted individual effort to integrate her own faith into the class. During reflection exercises in class, Amani journaled in Islamic principles or Qur'anic verses that she thought were relevant in the context. "My religion and spirituality are connected to feminist/decolonial/liberatory concepts," she told me, "So I was thinking about them jointly." She added, "Even when we were doing pre-show rituals and practices, a lot of my personal ones were *du'as* [supplications] and Qur'anic passages that I resonated with regarding racial, social, and environmental justice and what true liberatory futures look like—to me, true liberation especially for Black people and historically marginalized groups cannot happen in this *dunya* [world]. Justice will be served in the Afterlife."

For Amani then, normativity was monotheism per her Islamic beliefs, and she placed authority in God and the Qur'an. The conceptual framework of her course was completely counternormative in that the epistemological perspectives were grounded in polytheistic faiths and traditions. However, the course included other content that she found valuable—gender justice, liberation, decolonization—and identified with. She had to do the extra work of integrating her faith with these ideas, which, for her, was a mostly individual process. I asked her if there were any other Muslims in her class or if the guest speakers ever included a Muslim. "No," she answered, "but when we were asked to share our writings/drawings I would share out what I had and sometimes it would be those Qur'anic passages or principles that I mentioned."

Thus, Amani's personalization process was similar to Idris's and Amira's in that she exercised agency and autonomy vis-à-vis authority to create her own Muslim experience and engage Islam. However, her religious change was not one through which she altered her external alignments. (She did not, for example, drop the class; in fact, she very much loved the class). Her change had to do with changing the very epistemological framing of the class—she exercised autonomy and agency to find a creative way both to preserve her religious beliefs vis-à-vis monotheism and to benefit from the course content because it aligned with her moral politics. She did this successfully and very much on her own, and at first blush it appears to have been reflective of individualism. However, in her efforts to curate the class for herself she often referred to Allah (God), Qur'anic principles and passages, supplications, and Islamic eschatological frames (e.g., the Afterlife). This, again, is not an absolute individualism because she reverted to beliefs that she had grown up with ("that my parents taught me" as she once said) to ground her, while also taking from the class whatever she found beneficial. We can also understand this process in terms of Adhami's "faith as inheritance" framework, whereby American Muslims return to their upbringing or familial knowledge and culture on Islam as the default, in the face of uncertainty.[44] Amani similarly draws on her prior knowledge to ground her. Her personalization strategy, then, is one through which she imagines Islam to be broad enough to allow her to benefit from a class whose very foundation is rooted in polytheistic traditions. Ultimately, this allows her to live out her Muslimness in creative ways that work for her.

Conclusion

I began this chapter by highlighting the idea that scholars of religion and higher education make two opposing claims about religious change in college: either that it occurs, and beliefs individualize,[45] or that college has no impact and beliefs stay intact.[46] Through the case of Idris, Amira, and Amani and their respective personalization processes, I argue that we can understand religious change differently: namely, that some change can occur (such as altering external alignments or epistemological frames) and that beliefs can individualize in some ways, but that this process is ultimately motivated by and reinforces original beliefs. For this reason, I have offered personalization as the concept that encompasses their agency, autonomy, and relationship with authority—and thus the totality of these students' lived experiences on campus. Based on their unique and complex experiences as well as their respective personalization processes, we can derive conclusions about (1) religious engagement on campus and (2) individualism in general.

First, with regard to campus religious engagement, the lived experience of these Muslim students contradicts the trend that points toward college students' engagement being broad and not deep.[47] In fact, these cases show the opposite: the students' engagement with Islam, Islamic scripture, and Muslim life is quite deep. Relatedly, this means that these Muslim students do not "stow away" their identities in a "lockbox" only to return to them years later.[48] Rather, they are thoughtful about their choices and continue to invest their time and energies into engaging their faith, even if they do them in their own personalized ways.

In addition, their experiences also show that unlike the determinations made by Cherry et. al. that college reduces religious orthodoxy,[49] this is not the case for them. College, for them, does not necessarily have a liberalizing influence. Even Amira, who we might consider as being the most morally progressive is orthodox in her reference back to God and the Qur'an as sources of reconciliation and authority. This also tells us that these Muslim students' faith cannot also be categorized as what Smith and Denton call moral therapeutic deism" (MTD)—a faith that imagines the role of God to be a watchful, "on-call" entity that does not intervene in daily lives but is available when needed,[50] or what Flory and Denton also call a "Back-Pocket God."[51] Rather, for these students, God isn't in their back-pockets. He is more present and intervenes often, being a source of authority, reconciliation, or epistemological reference.

Second, the religious engagement of these Muslim students complements how they experience individualism. We learn from these student experiences that their individualism is not absolute in the Sheilaism sense.[52] This is so because of two reasons. First, they do not have the luxury of such absolutism due to their religio-racial minority status. That is, they are part of a religious and racialized demographic whose identity is inherently politicized, and therefore they cannot just inhabit the world as unmarked individuals with wholly subjective and private experiences of faith—in the way that Sheila Larson would. Second, their individualism is not absolute also because they continue to value some level of authority even as they exhibit features of individualism. Each of these students makes agentic and autonomous moves, but all of them also acknowledge the authority of God and the Qur'an in some form or another. In addition, even if they do not explicitly acknowledge it and even as they make some autonomous moves away from human religious authority, they do still place some level of trust in alternative religious authorities as long as their moral sensibilities do not contradict their own. Given their faith developmental stage, this would make sense: as James Fowler[53] and Sharon Parks[54] have noted; at this stage, students assume nothing about authority, but to some extent they still perceive it to be outside themselves. Parks explains that "authority is now more consciously 'chosen' by the young or emerging adult because the particular source of authority (now a more mentoring presence) makes sense in terms of the meaning-making of the emerging adults."[55] This choice, I argue, is indicative of autonomy in the sense that it is a move *away* from a particular authority even if it moves toward a different one.

Additionally, as Uecker and Froese have shown in their study of religious individualism and moral progressivism, "the hidden irony to moral individualism is that personal moral preferences remain largely a product of collective social forces. The difference is that popular moral attitudes are not codified in sacred texts or believed to be the sole domain of institutional authorities. Rather, they emanate from a cultural ether that communicates values through social networks and media in nonhierarchical ways."[56] In this regard, the experience of these students aligns with the finding that social networks, service attendance, and parental relationships have an influence on religious individualism.[57] One reason the individualism of these students is not absolute is precisely because they continue to stay connected to community in some ways, or, as Amani does, they revert to what they have been taught by their parents.

Finally, these students' experiences reveal that their individualism is not an artefact of a "deep cultural code" as imagined by Bellah but indeed a "strategy of action" as reimagined by O'Brien.[58] Given that Bellah's construction of individualism is rooted squarely in Protestant theology, it would make sense that the experiences of Muslim students would not neatly map on to it. Thus, their process of faith engagement is different from the way we typically understand religious individualism and instead better understood as personalization.

Ultimately, despite being embedded in a secular campus context with an enduring Protestant legacy that manifests in subtle and nuanced ways, these Muslim students, their lived experiences, and their personalization processes show us that religious engagement in college can take different forms for different communities and that Muslim students on campus not only passively experience such engagement differently but actively partake in curating it. Thus, even though their encounter of Islam on campus is mediated by Protestant–secular features and their Muslimness is boxed into binaries and categories, these Muslim students nevertheless exercise creative agency and autonomy to curate their experience on campus—to personalize it—so that Islam and being Muslim continues to make sense to them.

Conclusion

For a while during my fieldwork, I spent days shadowing individual students, during which I accompanied them to their classes whenever possible. One time, I was in a Political Science class with Kareem, where the instructor was discussing historical transitions to democracy. She was using the text *Democracy and Its Critics* by Robert A. Dahl,[1] and in this particular session she was explaining that the gradual evolution of democratic governance has its roots in competition among the elites. "When competition expands, participation does too."

A student asked for clarification, to which she replied: "Basically when we think about original forms of governance excluding women, non-property owners, racial groups, and so on—which is normatively atrocious of course—we can see how tolerating them would facilitate power for the elites, so they are not threatened by these groups. I'm not justifying this approach; I know I'm teaching a dated book but it's seminal in this field."

At this point, Kareem raised his hand, and the instructor nodded, encouraging him to speak. "I was wondering why we just can't have an inclusive political model that takes into account minorities."

"Can you elaborate on that? What do you mean?," the instructor probed.

"I mean why just tolerate? Why not go further and appoint them to positions in the government. Because, if minorities are already part of the government, they won't rebel, right?"

The instructor smiled and said, "Yes, exactly. That's an imaginative way to think about it, and as Lyndon Johnson said, 'I would

Being Muslim on Campus. Abiya Ahmed, Oxford University Press. © Oxford University Press 2026.
DOI: 10.1093/9780197773628.003.0006

rather have my opponents inside the tent spitting out than outside the tent spitting in.' "[2]

The instructor went on to discuss comparative politics and the development of global democracies. After class, I asked Kareem about his question and the instructor's response. "Yeah, I asked because she was talking about elites and power, and it just makes sense to incorporate minorities so they're no longer a threat, right? Like I just think it's interesting to think about not just who's in and who's out, but also why and how, right?"

Right. Early on in this book, I asked the following question: If the story of religion and secularity in the American context is riddled with Protestantism in many ways, what does that mean for non-Protestant Americans? To borrow from Lyndon Johnson again and Kareem, they are definitely "inside the tent" and "incorporated," but how are they doing? What are their experiences like inside the tent? What challenges and opportunities do they have?

The case of Muslim students, a religio-racial minority at Bellington University (BU), helps us answer these questions. BU Muslim students are embedded in a Protestant–secular context—representative of enduring elite power—that mediates their encounters of religion, Islam, and their lived Muslim experiences. We've explored what this looks like in terms of campus pluralism, privatization of religious beliefs, and personalization of lived experience, but more significantly, the case of Muslim students presents a critique of the categories of religion and secularity and also of institutional secularity and its role in mediating religious commitments.

The experience of these Muslim students on campus is complex. They encounter what they believe to be a secular campus, but they find religion embedded in it, often in unfamiliar ways. Their encounter with Islam and Muslim life is especially telling because their own ideas about Islam and their experiences of being Muslim do not neatly map onto notions of religion rooted in Protestant legacies. On campus, this means that students both appreciate the ritual accommodations offered to them (such as prayer spaces or Ramadan services) and critique the forms of public celebration of their faith (such as the Mawlid). Moreover, even in contexts that are presumably their own niches—such as the Muslim Student Association (MSA)—students encounter objectification of religion in ways that limit their ideas because these subcultures are a product of the very institutional context in which they are entrenched. In addition, Muslim students are acutely aware of the unspoken rules of bringing in religion into discourse, both broadly on campus and in smaller community settings.

However, as the last chapter indicates, they nevertheless make agentic and autonomous moves to personalize their lived Muslim experience on campus in ways that make sense to them. While this strategy is necessary for them given their religio-racial status and objectification of their Muslimness, it is also significant that these Muslims do not become Protestant, metaphorically speaking. G. K. Chesterton famously said, "in America, even the Catholics are Protestants,"[3] implying that all non-Protestants eventually adapt in form and function to the Protestant structure of American society or, to borrow from Porterfield, develop a Protestant orientation.[4] My encounters and experiences with these Muslim students show that this is not the case. For them, the place of religion at their campus is laden with complexity and historical legacies they might not necessarily fully understand or be able to articulate, but they nevertheless chart their course to be able to live Islam in ways that allow them to preserve a Muslim orientation or, rather, Muslim *orientations*. I use the plural because not only are the students' experiences complex, they themselves are also complex with diverse and fluid approaches to their religiosity, defying standard and binary conceptions of being a "certain type of Muslim." What unites them is their creative agency and their dedicated fidelity to Islam and Muslimness. Whether we attribute this to inherent resistance, to family and community ties, or to the fact that Islam, as a tradition, can be inclusive of various permutations of "religion," the case of these students shows that the place of religion on campus remains fraught and nuanced for some communities, even if they are "inside the tent."

What Now?

Let me conclude with where I started: the full circle of having begun primarily as a researcher of these issues to then also becoming a practitioner. Some readers might expect that I have groundbreaking alternatives or solutions to the challenges I have highlighted. I don't. Quite simply, my research led me to a gaping hole in the discourse and praxis of religion and secularity in higher education, whose contours and depth became evident through the case of BU Muslim students. My aim has been to make visible this hole and through it, related issues of institutional inclusion efforts and student agency.

What I *can* offer is that my own practice has benefited from this awareness. More specifically, I aim to prioritize students' agency and center their voices in the curation of programs and resources. I've found that this approach not only respects and empowers students but also strengthens their sense of belonging and contributes to their success. Moreover, with students and with colleagues too, I try not to miss an opportunity to interrogate the formations and applications of "religion" and "secularity." Sometimes this critical probing prompts puzzled looks ("What do you mean, religion with a capital R?"); but, more often than not, it sparks a moment of clarity: a realization that discourses and lenses of pervasive and dominant structures that we apply to other identity categories have not been sufficiently considered for religion and secularity on campus. And, if the last two years have taught us anything, it is that students' religion, religiosity, and religious experiences are deeply embedded in campus life, intersecting with politics, law, and culture in ways that challenge the status quo and call into question institutional inclusion initiatives.

Acknowledging these tensions and complexities can be liberating for all involved, but especially for students themselves. When they are aware of the terms of inclusion, they make informed choices about how they engage with their minority status and, in this case, with their religiosity. Indeed, the BU students show us that they *are* aware in some ways and that there are ways to be authentically Muslim even in constrained settings. They may not articulate it in disciplinary or theoretical terms, but their lived experience indicates that they are acutely attuned to institutional secularity and its derivatives intervening in their Muslimness, and they show us how to inhabit, navigate, and challenge this mediation by making space for themselves.

For the rest of us, this kind of agency is instructive. For one thing, it already defies the "oppressor–oppressed" binary that critics often use to undercut the case for acknowledging the role of power and privilege. There is no doubt that Islamophobia and other forms of racism and discrimination continue to be real and problematic factors at structural and individual scales, especially in the higher education context today.[5] But students like Amani or Idris or Ayesha neither see themselves as oppressed victims of Islamophobia nor consider their institution as oppressive or administrators as oppressors. At the same time, they are also not oblivious to the power structures and configurations, to the institutional container that tries to contain them and their religious commitments. They experience the Protestant *in* the secular. They recognize that those in privileged positions have incorporated them "inside the tent" on certain terms; but they also recognize that they have some agency within those terms. This acknowledgment of power and privilege helps them live authentically with fidelity to their religiosity. They do this without resorting to a "cancel culture" mode that is often expected of anyone grappling with structural power and privilege.

The students' agency is also instructive for professionals and practitioners—faculty, staff, administrators—who work with them and who set up substructures and programs for them. To what extent do these offerings center students and student needs? For example, we might ask the following question: How could a critical understanding of institutional Protestant–secularity and the power it wields inform the way Muslim chaplains do their work? Being situated within religious life offices, many chaplaincy models are a remnant of Protestant presence on campus, which necessarily limits the impact and freedom of Muslim (and likely other non-Protestant) chaplains. Similarly, how could other student affairs professionals—in residence units, admissions, multicultural, and equity/access offices—and others who serve such students – benefit from recognizing the role of Protestant–secularity in established policies and practices and in creating new ones? What about faculty and academic units that curate courses and events on religion and religious studies and inevitably set the boundaries of discourse within which students can participate? How about senior administrators and leaders who might at times collapse religious identity and experience into other categories and at other times highlight it as monolithic? These are all questions worth considering and move us toward improving the systems within which we work.

Practitioners are not the only group that should ask these questions; researchers should too. In this vein, by weaving together three core stories—the contradictions of institutional secularity, the limits of inclusion, and the agency of the students—I have attempted to respond to Small and Bowman's call that "This is the time to move away from generalizations and into more concrete specifics: What do different students do? What do they believe? And why?"[6] But I hope that this book serves only as a point of departure for other such investigations that detail the nuanced and complex picture of religious engagement on campus. It will be worthwhile, for example, to examine the intersectional experiences of an even broader range of ideologically and politically diverse Muslim and Muslim-adjacent students, especially with the spotlight on these populations after recent campus expressive activity beginning in 2023–2024.

Additionally, exploring the experiences of other minority religious communities—including those within various Christian denominations—vis-à-vis Protestant–secularity in higher education will also be instructive. Relatedly, the students at BU live on or around campus, so it is a specific context they inhabit because they are embedded in institutional Protestant–secularity in ways that those at a nonresidential campus are not. BU is also a well-resourced campus, which absolutely informs student services and experience. There are campuses parallel to BU which would perhaps mirror exactly these student experiences, but exploring other diverse sites—commuter colleges, liberal arts colleges, public universities—which might be at different points on the "Protestant–secular continuum"[7] will be critical in understanding the scope and impact of institutional secularity on various student populations and within different contexts.

Ultimately, as the case of BU students illustrates and reminds us, the more we understand and learn the systems and structures we are in, the more informed our choices will become as we function with and within them.

Acknowledgments

The Prophet Muhammad (peace and blessings be upon him) is reported to have said, "Whoever has not thanked people has not thanked God." In what follows I am mainly going to thank people; but, let me begin first with explicit gratitude to God: all Praise is for Him, Who gave me the privilege, opportunity, and ability to complete this project. Anything beneficial from this work is due to His Grace, and all shortcomings are because of my own limitations.

And now, for the people.

To the students who generously gave me their time and shared their lives—thank you. I hope you see yourself reflected here: that I did justice to your experiences, and that this is a book not just about you but *for* you.

To my colleagues and mentors who offered formal and informal feedback on this project or supported it in some way—Anthony Antonio, Zaid Adhami, Anna Bigelow, Benjamin Davidson, Cassie Garcia, Faith Kazmi, Salman Khan, Ari Y. Kelman, Alexander Key, Jonathan Rosa, Samuel Santos Jr., and Shirin Sinnar—thank you for your thoughtful engagement with parts or all of this book and your encouragement throughout. (Alexander, the "container" is in the record now!).

To my OUP editors, Theodore Calderara, Sofia Belimova, and others, as well as all the reviewers—thank you for your comments and critical feedback that helped make the final version what it is.

To Sana—thank you for your selflessness and reliability, for the laughs, and for being so much more than a friend. Everyone should experience a friendship this joyous and deep.

To Misha—for the phone calls sustaining my morning drives and for the two-decade-long friendship across continents and throughout the trajectory of our lives. Thank you.

To Ammi and Abboo—my parents—whose hard work, sacrifices, and *du'as* for me are, without a doubt, the reason for my successes. Thank you. I hope this makes you proud.

To Atif—my husband and mirror—whose partnership continues to ground me, and whose quiet steadiness and wry humor have often calmed my storms (even when I have failed to admit it!). For your love, care, and patience with me, but most importantly for believing in me, thank you.

To Ismael and Noor—my dearest children and greatest adventures—thank you for your unconditional love, wild imaginations, and infinite questions. You continue to remind me that *stories matter*, and I hope that this book reminds you both to never stop telling your own. May God always deepen your faith, increase your knowledge, sharpen your wisdom, beautify your character, and make you a source of *khayr* in this world. Ameen.

Notes

Introduction

1. In this book, when I use the term *Protestant* or *Protestant Christianity*, I mean mainline liberal Protestantism, and more, specifically, as Joshi has shown, it is white Protestant privilege that wields power both within Christianity and outside of it. See Kyathi Joshi, *White Christian Privilege* (New York University Press, 2020). Relatedly, on whiteness and secularity, as Vincent Lloyd has acutely observed, ". . . race and secularism are entwined. Put more starkly, whiteness is secular, and the secular is white. The unmarked racial category and the unmarked religious category jointly mark their others. Or, put another way, the desire to stand outside religion and the desire to stand outside race are complementary delusions, for the seemingly outside is in fact the hegemonic." See Vincent Lloyd, "Introduction," *Race and Secularism in America* (Columbia University Press, 2016).
2. All names of people and places, as well as those of the institution and its substructures, are pseudonyms. All historical facts and statistics on BU have been obtained through its founding grant, historical records, statistics provided by the Provost's Office, and articles written by scholars on its history. However, to protect the anonymity of the institution and those involved in this study, I have not cited these references.
3. George Marsden, *The Soul of the American University: From Protestant Establishment to Established Nonbelief* (Oxford University Press, 1994).
4. Douglas Jacobsen and Rhonda Jacobsen, *The American University in a Postsecular Age*, eds. (Oxford University Press, 2008); John Schmaulzbauer and Kathleen Mahoney, *The Resilience of Religion in American Education* (Baylor University Press, 2018). Marsden himself, updating his treatise two decades later, ends up contending with postsecularity in *The Soul of the American University Revisited* (Oxford University Press, 2021).
5. Eboo Patel, *Out of Many Faiths* (Princeton University Press, 2018).
6. Winnifred Sullivan, *The Impossibility of Religious Freedom* (Princeton University Press, 2018).
7. Courtney Bender and Ann Taves, eds., *What Matters? Ethnographies of Value in a Secular Age* (Columbia University Press, 2012).
8. Wendy Cadge and Mary Ellen Konieczny. "'Hidden in Plain Sight': The Significance of Religion and Spirituality in Secular Organizations." *Sociology of Religion* 75, no. 4 (2014): 551–63. https://doi.org/10.1093/socrel/sru043, 552-3.
9. Marsden, *Soul of the American University.*
10. C. John Sommerville, *The Decline of the Secular University* (Oxford University Press, 2006).
11. Douglas Jacobsen and Rhonda Jacobsen, *No Longer Invisible*: *Religion in University Education* (Oxford University Press, 2012).
12. Jacobsen and Jacobsen, *No Longer Invisible*, 13.

13. Talal Asad, *Formations of the Secular* (Stanford University Press, 2003); Sherman Jackson, *The Islamic Secular* (Oxford University Press, 2023).
14. See, for example, Tomoko Masuzawa, *The Invention of World Religions* (University of Chicago Press, 2005); Brent Nongbri, *Before Religion: A History of a Modern Concept* (Yale University Press, 2013); Janet Jakobsen and Ann Pellegrini, eds., *Secularisms* (Duke University Press, 2008); Jonathan Z. Smith, "Religion, Religions, Religious," in *Critical Terms for Religious Studies*, ed. Mark Taylor (University of Chicago Press 1998), 269–84.
15. Joshi, *White Christian Privilege;* Jenny L. Small, Sachi Edwards, Matthew R. Sayers, Renee L. Bowling, Julia R. Collett, Simran Kaur-Colbert, and J. Cody Nielsen, "Recognizing Christian Hegemony as Broader than Christian Privilege: Critical Religion Scholars Respond to Glanzer," *Religion & Education*, 49, no. 4 (2022): 355–73, https://doi.org/10.1080/15507394.2022.2139996.
16. Tracy Fessenden, *Culture and Redemption: Religion, the Secular, and American Literature* (Princeton University Press, 2007); Jakobsen and Pellegrini, *Secularisms.*
17. Andrew L Whitehead, Samuel L Perry, and Joseph O Baker, "Make America Christian Again: Christian Nationalism and Voting for Donald Trump in the 2016 Presidential Election," *Sociology of Religion*, 79, no. 2 (2018): 147–71, https://doi.org/10.1093/socrel/srx070; Nazita Lajevardi and Kassra A. R. Oskooii. "Old-Fashioned Racism, Contemporary Islamophobia, and the Isolation of Muslim Americans in the Age of Trump." *The Journal of Race, Ethnicity, and Politics*, 3, no. 1 (2018): 112–52. https://doi.org/10.1017/rep.2017.37.
18. Jonathan Rosa and Yarimar Bonilla, "Deprovincializing Trump, Decolonizing Diversity, and Unsettling Anthropology." *American Ethnologist*, 44, no. 2 (2017): 201–208. https://doi.org/10.1111/amet.12468, 204.
19. Dalia Mogahed, "Winning Muslim Votes: A Policy Priority Analysis in Swing States." *Institute of Social Policy and Understanding (ISPU)*, September 17, 2024, https://ispu.org/winning-muslim-votes-1/; Idris Umarji and Youssef Chouhoud, "American Muslims and the 2024 Election: Why American Muslims Are Rethinking Political Alliances." *Yaqeen Institute*, October 4, 2024, https://yaqeeninstitute.org/read/post/american-muslims-and-the-2024-election-why-american-muslims-are-rethinking-political-alliances.
20. Rosa and Bonilla, "Deprovincializing Trump," 204.
21. "The Dismantling of DEI," 2024. *Chronicle of Higher Education*, https://www.chronicle.com/package/the-assault-on-dei
22. Lilah Burke, "DEI at Public Colleges, Medical Schools Comes under Congressional Attack." *Higher Ed Dive*, March 7, 2024, https://www.highereddive.com/news/house-committee-hearing-dei-college-campuses/709684/.
23. Natasha Warikoo, *The Diversity Bargain: and Other Dilemmas of Race, Admissions, and Meritocracy at Elite Universities* (University of Chicago Press, 2016); Anthony Jack, *The Privileged Poor: How Elite Colleges Are Failing Disadvantaged Students* (Harvard University Press, 2019).
24. Evelyn Alsultany, *Broken: The Failed Promise of Muslim Inclusion* (New York University Press, 2022).
25. Stanford Muslim, Arab, and Palestinian Communities Committee, "Rupture and Repair." Stanford University, May 2024, https://news.stanford.edu/__data/assets/pdf_file/0031/156586/MAP-final-report-2024.pdf; Presidential Task Force on Combating Anti-Muslim and Anti-Arab Bias, "Preliminary Recommendations." Harvard University, June 24, 2024, https://www.harvard.edu/wp-content/uploads/2024/06/June-2024-preliminary-recommendations-AMAAB.pdf; UCLA Task Force on Anti-Palestinian, Anti-Arab, and Anti-Muslim Racism, University of California at

Los Angeles, https://uclaracismtaskforce.com/. See also Nancy Khalil, "How Campus Protests Exposed the Flaws in Higher Education Diversity Initiatives," *Middle East Eye*, September 2, 2024, https://www.middleeasteye.net/opinion/how-campus-protests-exposed-flaws-university-diversity-initiatives

26. Porterfield, "Religious Pluralism, the Study of Religion, and Postsecular Culture," in *The American University in a Postsecular Age*, Douglas Jacobsen and Rhonda Jacobsen, eds. (Oxford University Press, 2008), 196.
27. Shabana Mir, *Muslim American Women on Campus* (University of North Carolina Press, 2014).
28. Warikoo, *The Diversity Bargain*; Jack, *The Privileged Poor.*
29. Shaun Harper et al., "Truths about DEI on College Campuses"; USC Race and Equity Center, March 2024, https://race.usc.edu/wp-content/uploads/2024/03/Harper-and-Associates-DEI-Truths-Report.pdf
30. Khyati Y. Joshi, "DEI Is More than Race and Gender. It's Faith, Too."in *Religion News Service*, October 11, 2022, https://religionnews.com/2022/10/11/dei-is-more-than-race-and-gender-its-faith-too/.
31. Harper et al., "Truths about DEI," 14.
32. Caner Dagli, "Muslims Are not a Race" in *Renovatio*, February 6, 2020, https://renovatio.zaytuna.edu/article/muslims-are-not-a-race
33. Lane A. Glenn, "It's Time to Turn the Page on DEI," *Inside Higher Ed*, March 11, 2025, https://www.insidehighered.com/opinion/views/2025/03/11/its-time-turn-page-dei-opinion
34. Lori Peek, "Becoming Muslim: The Development of a Religious Identity." *Sociology of Religion*, 66 (2005): 215–42. http://www.jstor.org/stable/4153097
35. Na'ilah Suad Nasir and Jasiyah Al-Amin, "Creating Identity-Safe Spaces on College Campuses for Muslim Students." *Change: The Magazine of Higher Learning*, 38, no. 2 (2006): 22–27. https://doi.org/10.3200/CHNG.38.2.22-27
36. Shafiqa Ahmadi and Darnell Cole, eds., *Islamophobia in Higher Education: Combatting Discrimination and Creating Understanding* (Stylus Publishing, 2020); Shafiqa Ahmadi. "The Erosion of Civil Rights: Exploring the Effects of the Patriot Act on Muslims in American higher Education." *Rutgers Race and the Law Review*, 12, no. 1 (2011): 1–55. https://doi.org/10.1017/CBO9781107415324.004
37. Sameera Ahmed, Wahiba Abu-Ras, and Cynthia Arfken, "Prevalence of Risk Behaviors Among U.S. Muslim College Students," *Journal of Muslim Mental Health*, 8, no. 1 (2014): 5–19, https://doi.org/10.3998/jmmh.10381607.0008.101
38. Jeff Jensen Arnett. *Emerging Adulthood: The Winding Road from the Late Teens through the Twenties* (Oxford University Press, 2015).
39. Mir, *Muslim American Women on Campus.*
40. Mir, *Muslim American Women on Campus*, 4.
41. Mir, *Muslim American Women on Campus*, 5.
42. Marsden, *The Soul of the American University;* Sommerville, *The Decline of the Secular University.*
43. Jacobsen and Jacobsen, *No Longer Invisible*; Schmaulzbauer and Mahoney, *The Resilience of Religion.*
44. Marsden, *The Soul of the American University.*
45. All historical facts and statistics on BU have been obtained through its founding grant, historical records, statistics provided by the Provost's Office, and articles written by scholars on its history. However, to maintain the anonymity of the institution and those involved in this study, I have not cited these references.
46. Rabia Kamal, "American Muslim Youth Movements," *The Oxford Handbook of American Islam* (Oxford University Press, 2014); Kambiz GhaneaBassiri, *A History*

of Islam in America: From the New World to the New World Order (Cambridge University Press, 2010)

47. Lori Patton (eds.), *Cultural Centers in Higher Education: Perspectives on Identity, Theory, and Practice* (Routledge, 2011).
48. Omar Lizardo. "Improving Cultural Analysis: Considering Personal Culture in Its Declarative and Nondeclarative Modes," in *American Sociological Review*, 82, no. 1 (2017): 88–115.
49. Rachel Rinaldo and Jeffrey Guhin. "How and Why Interviews Work: Ethnographic Interviews and Meso-level Public Culture." *Sociological Methods & Research*, 51 no. 1 (2022): 34–67. https://doi.org/10.1177/0049124119882471
50. Rinaldo and Guhin, "How and Why Interviews Work," 14–15.
51. Judith Weisenfeld, *New World A-Coming: Black Religion and Racial Identity during the Great Migration* (New York University Press, 2017), 5.
52. See, for example: Sherman Jackson, *Islam and the Blackamerican: Looking Toward the Third Resurrection* (Oxford University Press, 2005); Zareena Grewal, *Islam Is a Foreign Country* (New York University Press, 2014); Ahmed Afzal, *Lone Star Muslims* (New York University Press, 2014); Su'ad Abdul-Khabeer, *Muslim Cool: Race, Religion, and Hip Hop in the United States* (New York University Press, 2016); Erik Love, *Islamophobia and Racism in America* (New York University Press, 2017); Sylvia Chan-Malik, *Being Muslim: A Cultural History of Women of Color in American Islam* (New York University Press, 2018); Harold D. Morales, *Latino and Muslim in America* (Oxford University Press, 2018).
53. See, for example, Tomoko Masuzawa, *The Invention of World Religions* (University of Chicago Press, 2005); Brent Nongbri, *Before Religion: A History of a Modern Concept* (Yale University Press, 2013); Janet Jakobsen and Ann Pellegrini, eds., *Secularisms* (Duke University Press, 2008); Charles McCreary and Jeffrey Wheatley. "The Protestant Secular in the Study of American Religion: Reappraisal and Suggestions" in *Religion*, 47, no. 2 (2017): 256–76.

Chapter 1

1. José Casanova, "The Secular and Secularisms." *Social Research* 76, no. 4 (2009): 1049–66. http://www.jstor.org/stable/40972201.
2. Talal Asad, *Genealogies of Religion* (Johns Hopkins University Press, 1993).
3. Casanova, "The Secular and Secularisms," 1051.
4. Charles Taylor, *A Secular Age* (Harvard University Press, 2007).
5. Taylor, *A Secular Age*, 3.
6. Casanova, "The Secular and Secularisms," 1053.
7. Taylor, *A Secular Age.*
8. Casanova, "The Secular and Secularisms," 1053.
9. Jose Casanova, *Public Religions in the Modern World* (University of Chicago Press, 1994).
10. Michael Warner offers a subtle but important distinction between secularity and secularism (the former as "background" and the latter as "specific positions against that background"). I find the distinction helpful but one that is unnecessary to make for this project. See Michael Warner, "Was Antebellum America Secular?," *The Immanent Frame*, October 2, 2012. https://tif.ssrc.org/2012/10/02/was-antebellum-america-secular/.
11. Saba Mahmood, *Religious Difference in a Secular Age: A Minority Report* (Princeton University Press, 2015).

12. Casanova, "The Secular and Secularisms," 1053.
13. Saba Mahmood, "Can Secularism Be otherwise?" in *Varieties of Secularism in a Secular Age*, ed. Michael Warner, Jonathan VanAntwerpen, and Craig Calhoun (Harvard University Press, 2010), 283.
14. Jonathan Z. Smith, "Religion, Religions, Religious" in *Critical Terms for Religious Studies*, ed. Mark Taylor (University of Chicago Press 1998), 269–84.
15. Asad, *Genealogies of Religion.*
16. See, for example, Mahmood, *Religious Difference;* Tomoko Masuzawa, *The Invention of World Religions* (University of Chicago Press, 2005); Brent Nongbri, *Before Religion: A History of a Modern Concept* (Yale University Press, 2013); Russell McCutcheon, *Manufacturing Religion: The Discourse on sui generis Religion and the Politics of Nostalgia* (Oxford University Press, 1997).
17. Janet Jakobsen and Ann Pellegrini, eds., *Secularisms* (Duke University Press, 2008), 8.
18. Nongbri, *Before Religion,* 18.
19. Nongbri, *Before Religion,* 18.
20. Mutakkabir and Nuriddin, *Religious Minority Students in Higher Education* (Routledge, 2016).
21. Winnifred Sullivan, *The Impossibility of Religious Freedom* (Princeton University Press, 2018).
22. Asma Uddin has illustrated how reducing Islam to a set of beliefs and practices offers an incomplete picture of Muslims' experiences with faith, especially in a Western context. See Asma Uddin, (Beacon Press, 2020).
23. Warner, VanAntwerpen, and Calhoun, *Varieties of Secularism,* 15.
24. John Modern, *Secularism in Antebellum America* (University of Chicago Press, 2011), 5.
25. Taylor, *A Secular Age.*
26. Peter Berger, *The Sacred Canopy: Elements of a Sociological Theory of Religion* (Anchor Books, 1967).
27. Modern, *Secularism in Antebellum America,* 114.
28. Tracy Fessenden, *Culture and Redemption: Religion, the Secular, and American Literature,* (Princeton University Press, 2007).
29. Fessenden, *Culture and Redemption,* 5.
30. Amanda Porterfield, *The Transformation of American Religion* (Oxford University Press, 2001).
31. Porterfield, *The Transformation of American Religion,* 7.
32. Masuzawa, *The Invention of World Religions,* 185.
33. See John R. Thelin, *A History of American Higher Education* (Johns Hopkins University Press, 2004); Richard Hofstadter and Walter P. Metzger, *The Development of Academic Freedom in the United States* (Columbia University Press, 1955); Fredrick Rudolph, *The American College and University: A History* (University of Georgia Press, 1962); Christian Smith, *The Secular Revolution: Power, Interests, and Conflict in the Secularization of American Public Life* (University of California Press, 2003); George Marsden, *The Soul of the American University: From Protestant Establishment to Established Nonbelief* (Oxford University Press, 1994); Julie A. Reuben, *The Making of the Modern University* (University of Chicago Press, 1996).
34. John Schmaulzbauer and Kathleen Mahoney, *The Resilience of Religion in American Education* (Baylor University Press, 2018).
35. Douglas Jacobsen and Rhonda H. Jacobsen, "Religion in Mainline and Independent Private Higher Education" in *The Oxford Handbook of Religion and American Education,* eds. Michael Waggoner and Nathan C. Walker (Oxford University Press, 2018), 312.

36. Jacobsen and Jacobsen, "Religion in Mainline and Independent Private Higher Education."
37. Khyati Joshi, *White Christian Privilege: The Illusion of Religious Equality in America* (New York University Press, 2020).
38. Marsden, *Soul of the American University*, 121.
39. Smith, *Secular Revolution*, 2–3.
40. Marsden, *Soul of the American University*.
41. Porterfield, *The Transformation of American Religion*, 199.
42. See Smith, *Secular Revolution*; Marsden, *Soul of the American University*; or Schmalzbauer and Mahoney, *The Resilience of Religion in American Education*.
43. Marsden, *Soul of the American University*, 156
44. Tomoko Masuzawa, "Secular by Default? Religion and the University before the Post-Secular Age," in *The Post-Secular in Question*, eds. Philip Gorski, David Kyuman Kim, John Torpey, and Jonathan VanAntwerpen (New York University Press, 2012), 185–214.
45. Schmaulzbauer and Mahoney, *The Resilience of Religion in American Education*, 28; see also D. G. Hart, *The University Gets Religion: Religious Studies in American Higher Education* (Johns Hopkins University Press, 1999); and Porterfield, *The Transformation of American Religion*.
46. Smith, *Secular Revolution*; Marsden, *Soul of the American University*.
47. Sarah Imhoff, "The Creation Story, or How We Learned to Stop Worrying and Love Schempp." *Journal of the American Academy of Religion*, 84, no. 2 (2016): 466–97.
48. Russell McCutcheon, "'Just Follow the Money: The Cold War, the Humanistic Study of Religion, and the Fallacy of Insufficient Cynicism." *Culture and Religion*, 5, no. 1 (2004): 41–69.
49. McCutcheon, "Just Follow the Money," 56.
50. Imhoff, "The Creation Story," 492.
51. George Marsden, *The Soul of the American University Revisited: From Protestant to Postsecular* (Oxford University Press, 2021).
52. Masuzawa, *The Invention of World Religions*.
53. Thelin, *A History of American Higher Education*; David Labaree, *A Perfect Mess* (University of Chicago Press, 2017).
54. Imhoff, "The Creation Story"; Lucia Hulsether, "The Grammar of Racism: Religious Pluralism and the Birth of the Interdisciplines," *Journal of the American Academy of Religion*, 86, no. 1 (2018): 1–41, https://doi.org/10.1093/jaarel/lfx049
55. Robert Wuthnow, "Can Faith Be More Than a Side Show in the Contemporary Academy?" in *The American University in a Postsecular Age*, eds. Douglas Jacobsen and Rhonda Jacobsen (Oxford University Press, 2008), 31–44.
56. Wuthnow, "Can Faith Be More Than a Side Show," 35.
57. Wuthnow, "Can Faith Be More Than a Side Show," 35.
58. Jon H. Roberts and James Turner, *The Sacred and the Secular University* (Cambridge University Press, 2000).
59. Wuthnow, "Can Faith Be More Than a Side Show," 37.
60. Warren Nord. *Does God Make a Difference? Taking Religion Seriously in Our Schools and Universities* (Oxford University Press, 2010), 75.
61. American Academy of Religion, AAR Religious Literacy Guidelines, October 3, 2019, https://aarweb.org/resource/aar-religious-literacy-guidelines-2/
62. Imhoff, "The Creation Story."
63. Sharon Parks, *Big Questions, Worthy Dreams: Mentoring Young Adults in Their Search for Meaning, Purpose, and Faith* (John Wiley & Sons, 2000). Jeff J. Arnett, *Emerging Adulthood: The Winding Road from the Late* (Oxford University

Press, 2015); Alexander W. Astin, Helen S. Astin, and Jennifer A. Lindholm, *Cultivating the Spirit: How College Can Enhance Students' Inner Lives* (Jossey-Bass, 2011).

64. Gorski et al., *The Post-Secular in Question* (New York University Press, 2012).
65. Wuthnow, "Can Faith Be More Than a Side Show," 39.
66. Douglas Jacobsen and Rhonda Jacobsen, *No Longer Invisible: Religion in University Education* (Oxford University Press, 2012).
67. Schmaulzbauer and Mahoney, *Resilience of Religion in American Education;* Eboo Patel, *Out of Many Faiths* (Princeton University Press, 2018).
68. Marsden, *The Soul of the American University Revisited*, 356.
69. Gorski et al., *The Post-Secular in Question.*
70. Gorski et al., *The Post-Secular in Question*, 2.
71. Gorski et al, *The Post-Secular in Question*, 2.
72. Jacobsen and Jacobsen, *No Longer Invisible; The American University in a post-secular age.*
73. Marsden, *The Soul of the American University Revisited*, 348.
74. Fessenden, *Culture and Redemption*; Jakobsen & Pellegrini, *Secularisms.*
75. Fessenden, *Culture and Redemption*
76. Charles McCreary and Jeffrey Wheatley, "The Protestant Secular in the Study of American Religion: Reappraisal and Suggestions" in *Religion*, 47, no. 2 (2017): 256–76.
77. McCreary and Wheatley, "The Protestant Secular," 259.
78. McCreary and Wheatley, "The Protestant Secular," 259.
79. See, for example, Jenny L. Small, *Understanding College Students' Spiritual Identities: Different Faiths, Varied Worldviews* (Hampton Press, 2011); Tricia Seifert, "Understanding Christian Privilege." *About Campus*, 12, no. 2 (2007): 10–17. https://doi.org/10.1002/abc.206; Scott Muir, "The Adhan Controversy in Historical Perspective: Interpenetrating Protestant, Secular, and Pluralist Paradigms at Duke University, 1839–2016." in *Journal of Religion and Society*, 19 (2017): 1–22; Warren Blumenfeld, "Challenging Christian Hegemony and Christian Privilege in Academia" in *Handbook on Promoting Social Justice in Education*, ed. R. Papa (Springer, 2019) https://doi.org/10.1007/978-3-319-74078-2_113-1.
80. See, for example, Michal J. Cuyjet, Mary F. Howard-Hamilton, and Diane L. Cooper, eds., *Multiculturalism on Campus: Theories, Models and Practices for Understanding Diversity and Creating Inclusion* (Stylus Publishing 2011); Marcia B. Baxter Magolda, "Three Elements of Self-Authorship." *Journal of College Student Development* 49, no. 4 (2008): 269–84. https://dx.doi.org/10.1353/csd.0.0016; and Astin, Astin, and Lindholm, *Cultivating the Spirit.*
81. Perry L. Glanzer, "Recognizing Christian Complexity and Secular Privilege in Higher Education: A Response to Recent Christian Privilege Arguments," in *Religion & Education*, 49 no. 2 (2022): 119–37, https://doi.org/10.1080/15507394.2022.2051973; Perry L. Glanzer and Jessica Martin, "Recognizing the "Both-And" instead of Promulgating the "Either-Or": A Critical Response to Critical Religion Scholars," in *Religion & Education*, 50. no.4 (2023): 232–45, https://doi.org/10.1080/15507394.2023.2245942
82. Jenny L. Small, Sachi Edwards, Matthew R. Sayers, Renee L. Bowling, Julia R. Collett, Simran Kaur-Colbert, and J. Cody Nielsen, "Recognizing Christian Hegemony as Broader than Christian Privilege: Critical Religion Scholars Respond to Glanzer," *Religion & Education*, 49, no. 4 (2022): 355–73, https://doi.org/10.1080/15507394.2022.2139996; Sachi Edwards, Jenny L. Small, Matthew R. Sayers, and Simran Kaur-Colbert, "One More Thing": Clarifying the Evidence

around Christian Privilege in Higher Education, *Religion & Education*, 50, no. 4 (2023): 246–56.

83. Joshi, *White Christian Privilege.*
84. David Sehat, *The Myth of American Religious Freedom* (Oxford University Press, 2011); Gordon Maples, Leah Rediger Wilson, and Jenny L. Small, "Privilege as Policy? An Analysis of Student Religious Accommodation Policies in Higher Education," *Journal of College and Character*, 22 (2021): 272–90, https://doi.org/10.1080/2194587X.2021.1977151
85. Walter Blumenfeld, "Christian Privilege and the Promotion of the"Secular" and Not-so "Secular" Mainline Christianity in Public Schooling and in the Larger Society," *Equity & Excellence in Education*, 39, no. 3 (2006): 195–210, https://doi.org/10.1080/10665680600788024; Joshi, *White Christian Privilege.*
86. Small et al., "Recognizing Christian Hegemony," 361
87. Asad, *Genealogies of Religion*; Fenella Cannell, "The Anthropology of Secularism," *Annual Review of Anthropology* 39 (2010): 85–100, https://doi.org/10.1146/annurev.anthro.012809.105039.

Chapter 2

1. Diana Eck, "Prospects for Pluralism: Voice and Vision in the Study of Religion." *Journal of the American Academy of Religion* 75, no. 4 (2007): 743–76. https://muse.jhu.edu/article/228403.
2. Eck, "Prospects for Pluralism," 245.
3. Eboo Patel and Cassie Meyer, "The Civic Relevance for Interfaith Cooperation for Colleges and Universities." *Journal of College and Character*, 12, no. 1 (2011): 2, https://doi:10.2202/1940-1639.1764.
4. Courtney Bender and Pamela Klassen, *After Pluralism: Reimagining Religious Engagement* (Columbia University Press, 2010), 3.
5. Eboo Patel, *Out of Many Faiths* (Princeton University Press, 2018).
6. Martin Marty, *The Protestant Voice in American Pluralism* (University of Georgia Press, 2004).
7. Marty, *The Protestant Voice in American Pluralism*, 67.
8. Amanda Porterfield, *The Transformation of American Religion* (Oxford University Press, 2001).
9. Porterfield, *The Transformation of American Religion*, 57.
10. Porterfield, *The Transformation of American Religion*, 57.
11. Robert P. Jones, "The Challenge of Pluralism after the End of White Christian America," in Eboo Patel, *Out of Many Faiths* (Princeton University Press, 2018), 113–32.
12. Jones, "The Challenge of Pluralism," 125.
13. Will Herberg, *Protestant-Catholic-Jew: An Essay in American Religious Sociology* (University of Chicago Press, 1983).
14. Herberg, *Protestant-Catholic-Jew.*
15. Robert N. Bellah, "Civil Religion in America," *Daedalus* 96, no. 1 (1967): 1–21. http://www.jstor.org/stable/20027022.
16. Porterfield, "Religious Pluralism, the Study of Religion, and Postsecular Culture," in *The American University in a Postsecular Age*, eds. Douglas Jacobsen and Rhonda Jacobsen (Oxford University Press, 2008), 196.
17. George Marsden, *The Soul of the American University Revisited* (Oxford University Press, 2021).

18. Ronit Stahl, "A Jewish America and a Protestant Civil Religion: Will Herberg, Robert Bellah, and Mid-Twentieth Century American Religion," *Religions* 6 (2015), 434–50. https://doi:10.3390/rel6020434
19. Herberg *Protestant-Catholic-Jew*, 257–58.
20. Patel, *Out of Many Faiths.*
21. Stahl, "A Jewish America and a Protestant Civil Religion," 447.
22. Eck, "Prospects for Pluralism," 259.
23. Marty, *The Protestant Voice in American Pluralism.*
24. Diana Eck and Brendan Randall, "Pluralism in Religion and American Education" in *The Oxford Handbook of Religion and American Education*, eds. Michael D. Waggoner and Nathan C. Walker (Oxford University Press, 2018).
25. Patel, *Out of Many Faiths.*
26. Patel, *Out of Many Faiths*, 70.
27. Denise A. Spellberg, "Could a Muslim Be President? An Eighteenth-Century Constitutional Debate." *Eighteenth-Century Studies* 39, no. 4 (2006): 485–506. http://www.jstor.org/stable/30053706.
28. Hypothetical because the Muslim identities of African slaves brought to America were not considered. Historians trace the presence of Islam in America as early as the fourteenth century (see, for example, Kambiz Ghaneabassiri, *A History of Islam in America*, Cambridge University Press, 2012).
29. Spellberg, "Could a Muslim Be President?," 502.
30. Patel, *Out of Many Faiths*, 42–44.
31. Rosemary Hicks, "Religious Pluralism, Secularism, and Interfaith Endeavors," in *The Cambridge Companion to American Islam*, ed. Juliane Hammer and Omid Safi (Cambridge: Cambridge University Press, 2013), 158.
32. Bender and Klassen, *After Pluralism.*
33. Hicks, 159.
34. William Hutchinson, *Religious Pluralism in America: The Contentious History of an American Ideal* (Yale University Press, 2004).
35. John Inazu, "Hope without a Common Good," in Patel, *Out of Many Faiths*, 148.
36. As Blumenfeld (2006) writes, there is "a hierarchy or continuum of Christian privilege based on (1) historical factors, (2) numbers of practitioners, and (3) degrees of social power" (2006, 195). White Protestants thus may have greater degrees of Christian privilege than some minority Christians—for example, African American and Latino/a churches, Amish, Mennonites, and Quakers.
37. Inazu, "Hope without a Common Good," 148.
38. Robert N. Bellah, "The Protestant Structure of American Culture," *The Hedgehog Review* 4 no. 1 (2002): 16.
39. Peter Berger, "Pluralism, Protestantization, and the Voluntary Principle" in *The New Sociology of Knowledge: The Life and Work of Peter L. Berger* (Transaction Publishers, 2013).
40. Patel, *Out of Many Faiths.*
41. "The Dismantling of DEI," 2024. *Chronicle of Higher Education*, https://www.chronicle.com/package/the-assault-on-dei
42. See, for example, Jenny Stuber, *Inside the College Gates: How Class and Culture Matter in Higher Education* (Lexington Books, 2011); Ann L. Mullen, *Degrees of Inequality* (Johns Hopkins University Press, 2010); Anthony Lising Antonio, "Diversity and the Influence of Friendship Groups in College." *The Review of Higher Education* 25, no. 1 (2001): 63–89. https://dx.doi.org/10.1353/rhe.2001.0013;
43. Anthony Abraham Jack, "Elite Colleges Are More Diverse Than Ever. They're Still Unequal" in *The Chronicle of Higher Education*; August 23, 2024, https://www.chronicle.com/article/elite-colleges-are-more-diverse-than-ever-theyre-still-unequal

44. See, for example, Alexander W. Astin, Helen S. Astin, and Jennifer A. Lindholm, *Cultivating the Spirit: How College Can Enhance Students' Inner Lives* (Jossey-Bass, 2011); Alyssa Bryant Rockenbach and Matthew Mayhew, *Spirituality in College Students' Lives: Translating Research into Practice* (Routledge, 2013); M. M. Kocet and D. L. Stewart, "The Role of Student Affairs in Promoting Religious and Secular Pluralism and Interfaith Cooperation." *Journal of College and Character*, 12, no. 1 (2011): 1–10. https://doi.org/10.2202/1940-1639.1762
45. Jacobsen and Jacobsen, *No Longer Invisible.*
46. Patel, *Out of Many Faiths*, 29.
47. Alyssa Rockenbach, Matthew J. Mayhew, Shauna Morin, Rebecca E. Crandall, and Ben Selznick, "Fostering the Pluralism Orientation of College Students through Interfaith Co-curricular Engagement." *The Review of Higher Education*, 39, no. 1 (2015): 25–58.
48. Nicholas Bowman and Jenny Small, "The Experiences and Spiritual Growth of Religiously Privileged and Religiously Marginalized College Students," in *Spirituality in College Students' Lives,* eds. Alyssa Rockenbach and Matthew J. Mayhew (Routledge 2012), 72.
49. Bret E. Carroll, "Spatial Politics and American Religious Pluralism," in *Oxford Research Encyclopedia of Religion*, April 26, 2017; Accessed March 25, 2025. https://oxfordre.com/religion/view/10.1093/acrefore/9780199340378.001.0001/acrefore-9780199340378-e-468.
50. Eck, "Prospect of Pluralism."
51. Wendy Cadge, *Spiritual Care: The Everyday Work of Chaplains* (Oxford University Press, 2022).
52. Sophie Gilliat-Ray, *Religion in Higher Education: The Politics of the Multi-Faith Campus* (Routledge, 2019).
53. Rose Aslan, *Muslim Prayer in American Public Life* (Oxford University Press, 2024).
54. Karla Johnson and Peter Laurence, "Multi-Faith Religious Spaces on College and University Campuses." *Religion and Education* 39, no. 1 (2012): 48–63; Alyssa Bryant, "Exploring Religious Pluralism in Higher Education: Non- Majority Religious Perspectives among Entering First-Year Students." *Religion and Education*, 33, No. 1 (2006): 1–25. https://doi.org/10.1080/15507394.2006.1001236; Patricia Karlin-Neumann and Joanne Sanders, "Bringing Faith to Campus: Religious and Spiritual Space, Time, and Practice at Stanford University." *Journal of College and Character*, 14, no. 2 (2013): 125–32.
55. Gilliat-Ray, *Religion in Higher Education*, 288.
56. Matthew J. Mayhew, Nicholas A. Bowman, and Alyssa Bryant Rockenbach, "Silencing Whom? Linking Campus Climates for Religious, Spiritual, and Worldview Diversity to Student Worldviews." *The Journal of Higher Education*, 85, no. 2 (2014): 240–41.
57. Alyssa N. Bryant, "Ecumenical Worldview Development by Gender, Race, and Worldview: A Multiple-Group Analysis of Model Invariance." *Research in Higher Education*, 52, no. 5 (2011): 460–79. http://www.jstor.org/stable/41483797.
58. Patel, *Out of Many Faiths.*
59. Hadia Mubarak, "How Muslim Students Negotiate Their Religious Identity and Practices in an Undergraduate Setting." *The Religious Engagement of American Undergraduates*, Social Science Research Council, 8 May 2007.
60. Tricia Seifert, "Understanding Christian Privilege." *About Campus*, 12, no. 2 (2007): 10–17. https://doi.org/10.1002/abc.206; Joshi, *White Christian Privilege.*
61. Gilliat-Ray, *Religion in Higher Education*, 304–305.
62. Robert Nash, *Religious Pluralism in the Academy: Opening the Dialogue* (Peter Lang Publishing, 2011).

63. Patel, *Out of Many Faiths*, 28.
64. *Tala'al badru 'alayna*, or "The full moon rose over us," is an Islamic poem that the residents of Madinah are reported to have recited for the Prophet Muhammad upon his arrival to Madinah, to welcome him and mark the culmination of his migration from Makkah.
65. Rhys Williams and Gira Vashi, "Hijab and American Muslim Women: Creating the Space for Autonomous Selves." *Sociology of Religion*, 68, no. 3 (2007): 269–287. https://www.jstor.org/stable/20453164
66. Nash, *Religious Pluralism in the Academy*, 43.
67. Nash, *Religious Pluralism in the Academy*, 43.
68. Shafiqa Ahmadi and Darnell Cole, eds., *Islamophobia in Higher Education* (Stylus Publishing, 2020); Musbah Shaheen, "Islamophobia in Higher Education Environments," *New Directions for Higher Education* 206 (2024): 41–52; Evelyn AlSultany, "Antisemitism and Islamophobia: The University's Diversity, Equity, Inclusion Response to October 7, 2023." *Journal of Palestine Studies*, 53, no. 4: 8–24. https://doi.org/10.1080/0377919X.2025.2455077
69. Riyad Ahmed Shahjahan, "Toward a Spiritual Praxis: The Role of Spirituality among Faculty of Color Teaching for Social Justice." *The Review of Higher Education*, 33, no.4 (2010): 473–512; Walter Blumenfeld, "Christian privilege and the promotion of the "secular" and not-so "secular" mainline Christianity in public schooling and in the larger society," *Equity and Excellence in Education*, 39, no. 3 (2006): 195–210, https://doi.org/10.1080/10665680600788024; Christine Clark, Mark Brimhall Vargas, Lewis Schlosser, and Craig Alimo. "Diversity Initiatives in Higher Education: It's Not Just "Secret Santa" in December: Addressing Educational and Workplace Climate Issues Linked to Christian Privilege." *Multicultural Education* 10, no. 2 (2002): 52–57. https://www.proquest.com/scholarly-journals/diversity-initiatives-higher-education-not-just/docview/216308802/se-2.
70. *Bid'ah*—an Arabic term for innovation. In religious terms, it is usually referred to as an innovation in Islam that is not sanctioned or encouraged or frowned upon. The Mawlid—or celebrating the birthday of the Prophet Muhammad—is considered to be a *bid'ah* by a significant group of Muslims.
71. Carroll, "Spatial Politics and American Religious Pluralism"; Cadge, *Spiritual Care*; Gilliat Ray, *Religion in Higher Education*.
72. Qanun is a harp-like instrument played in the Middle East, West Africa, Central Asia, and parts of Europe. The darbuka is a goblet drum associated primarily with Egypt, but also used in the Middle East, North Africa, South Asia, and Europe.
73. A form of Sufi Islamic singing popular in Pakistan, India, and parts of the Indian Sub-Continent.
74. Eck, "Prospects for Pluralism".
75. Jenny Small, *Critical Religious Pluralism in Higher Education* (Routledge, 2020), 7.
76. Marcia Hermansen, "Milad/Mawlid: Celebrating the Prophet Muhammad's Birthday" in *The Practice of Islam in America*, ed. Edward Curtis (New York University Press: 2017).
77. Bender and Klassen, *After Pluralism*, 16.
78. Small, *Critical Religious Pluralism*.
79. Porterfield, "Religious Pluralism, the Study of Religion, and Postsecular Culture," 192.
80. Porterfield, "Religious Pluralism, the Study of Religion, and Postsecular Culture," 193.
81. "Diversity, Equity, and Inclusion Initiatives with Brian Lowery, Iván Marinovic, and Eboo Patel"; Democracy and Disagreement 2024, https://humsci.stanford.edu/events/2025-02-11/diversity-equity-and-inclusion-initiatives-brian-lowery-ivan-marinovic-and-eboo

82. Danielle Allen, "How to Be a Confident Pluralist," Diversity Forum, University of Wisconsin-Madison, November 14, 2023, https://diversityforum.wisc.edu/session/danielle-allen-keynote/
83. "The Dismantling of DEI," in *Chronicle of Higher Education.*
84. Paul Brest and Emily J. Levine, "D.E.I. Is Not Working on College Campuses. We Need a New Approach," *New York Times*, August 30, 2024, https://www.nytimes.com/2024/08/30/opinion/college-dei-programs-diversity.html
85. Brest and Levine, ""D.E.I. Is Not Working on College Campuses."
86. Bender and Klassen, *After Pluralism*, 11.
87. Eck, "Pluralism: Problems and Promise," 9.
88. Jones, "The Challenge of Pluralism."
89. Bender and Klassen, *After Pluralism*, 68.
90. Small, *Critical Religious Pluralism.*

Chapter 3

1. Courtney Bender and Pamela Klassen, *After Pluralism: Reimagining Religious Engagement* (Columbia University Press, 2010); Tricia Seifert, "Understanding Christian Privilege," *About Campus*, 12, no. 2 (2007): 10–17. https://doi.org/10.1002/abc.206; Jenny Small, *Critical Religious Pluralism in Higher Education* (Routledge, 2020).
2. Rachel Rinaldo and Jeffrey Guhin, "How and Why Interviews Work: Ethnographic Interviews and Meso-level Public Culture," *Sociological Methods & Research*, 51 no. 1 (2022): 34–67. https://doi.org/10.1177/0049124119882471
3. Tracy Fessenden, *Culture and Redemption: Religion, the Secular, and American Literature* (Princeton University Press, 2007).
4. Charles Taylor, *A Secular Age* (Harvard University Press, 2007); José Casanova, "The Secular and Secularisms," *Social Research*, 76, no. 4 (2009): 1049–66. http://www.jstor.org/stable/40972201; José Casanova, *Public Religions in the Modern World* (University of Chicago Press, 1994).
5. Douglas Jacobsen and Rhonda Jacobsen, *The American University in a P* (Oxford University Press, 2008); Douglas Jacobsen and Rhonda Jacobsen, *No Longer Invisible: Religion in University Education* (Oxford University Press, 2012).
6. Tomoko Masuzawa, *The Invention of World Religions* (University of Chicago Press, 2005); Brent Nongbri, *Before Religion: A History of a Modern Concept* (Yale University Press, 2013); Winnifred Sullivan, *The Impossibility of Religious Freedom* (Princeton University Press, 2018).
7. Janet Jakobsen and Ann Pellegrini, eds., *Secularisms* (Duke University Press, 2008), 11.
8. Jakobsen and Pellegrini, eds., *Secularisms.*
9. Khaled Beydoun, *American Islamophobia* (University of California Press, 2018).
10. Masuzawa, *The Invention of World Religions*; Russell McCutcheon, "'Just Follow the Money': The Cold War, the Humanistic Study of Religion, and the Fallacy of Insufficient Cynicism." '*Culture and Religion*, 5, no. 1 (2004): 41–69.
11. Samuel Speers, "The Secular Thesis Revisited: Religious Life on the Secular College Campus Today." *Journal of College and Character*, 10, no. 1 (2008): 5. https://doi.org/10.2202/1940-1639.1056
12. Ahmed Abiya. "Muslim Student Associations in North America." *Oxford Research Encyclopedia of Religion*, April 16, 2025; accessed September 17, 2025. https://doi.

org/10.1093/acrefore/9780199340378.013.867; Kambiz Ghaneabassiri, *A History of Islam in America* (Cambridge University Press, 2012); Rabia Kamal, "American Muslim Youth Movements," *The Oxford Handbook of American Islam* (Oxford University Press, 2014); Sally Howell, "Laying the Groundwork for American Muslim Histories: 1865–1965," in *The Cambridge Companion to American Islam*, edited by Juliane Hammer and Omid Safi, 45–64 (Cambridge University Press, 2013).

13. Ghaneabassiri, *A History of Islam in America*, 266–67.
14. Justine Howe, "*Da'wa* in the Neighborhood: Female-Authored Muslim Students Association Publications, 1963–1980" in *Religion and American Culture: A Journal of Interpretation*, 29, no. 3 (2020): 291–325.
15. Howe, "*Da'wa* in the Neighborhood," 292.
16. Ahmed, "Muslim Student Associations in North America"; Zareena Grewal, *Islam Is a Foreign Country* (New York University Press, 2014); John Schmaulzbauer and Kathleen Mahoney. *The Resilience of Religion in American Education* (Baylor University Press, 2018).
17. Kamal, "American Muslim Youth Movements," 4.
18. Shabana Mir, *Muslim American Woman on Campus* (University of North Carolina Press, 2009), 245.
19. Timur Yuskaev, "Muslim Public Intellectuals and Global Muslim Thought," in *The Cambridge Companion to American Islam*, edited by Juliane Hammer and Omid Safi. (Cambridge University Press, 2013), 272.
20. Ghaneabassiri, *A History of Islam in America*; Howell, "Laying the Groundwork"; Howe ""*Da'wa* in the Neighborhood"; Mir, *Muslim American Women on Campus*, Kamal, "American Muslim Youth Movements."
21. Zaid Adhami, " (PhD diss., Duke University, 2017), 92. Duke Libraries. https://hdl.handle.net/10161/16368
22. Talal Asad, *Formations of the Secular* (Stanford University Press, 2003), 185.
23. Asad, *Formations of the Secular*, 185.
24. All names are pseudonyms.
25. Asad, *Formations of the Secular.*
26. Juliane Hammer, *American Muslim Women, Religious Authority, and Activism: More than a Prayer* (University of Texas Press, 2012).
27. Jonathan Brown, *Misquoting Muhammad: The Challenge and Choices of Interpreting the Prophet's Legacy* (Oneworld Publications, 2014).
28. Jacobsen and Jacobsen, *No Longer Invisible.*
29. McCutcheon, "'Just Follow the Money'"; Masuzawa, *Inventions of World Religions*; Sarah Imhoff, "The Creation Story, or How We Learned to Stop Worrying and Love Schempp." *Journal of the American Academy of Religion*, 84, no. 2 (2016): 466–497.
30. Sullivan, *Impossibility of Religious Freedom.*
31. Jakobsen and Pellegrini, *Secularisms.*
32. Asad, *Formations of the Secular.*
33. Ghaneabassiri, *A History of Islam in America*; Howell, "Laying the Groundwork"; Howe ""*Da'wa* in the Neighborhood"; Mir, *Muslim American Women on Campus*; Kamal, "American Muslim Youth Movements."
34. Mir, *Muslim American Women on Campus.*
35. Adhami, "Faith with Doubt."
36. Jakobsen and Pellegrini, *Secularisms.*
37. Asad, *Formations of the Secular.*
38. Jakobsen and Pellegrini, *Secularisms.*
39. Jacobsen and Jacobsen, *No Longer Invisible.*
40. Amy Binder and Kate Wood, *Becoming Right: How Campuses Shape Young Conservatives*, (Princeton University Press, 2013).

41. Mir, *Muslim American Women on Campus*, 241.
42. Salua Fawzi, "Experiencing Islam in America: Muslim Students Associations" (PhD diss., McGill University, 2019). https://escholarship.mcgill.ca/concern/theses/sj139422t
43. Grewal, *Islam Is a Foreign Country*, 321.
44. Sullivan, *Impossibility of Religious Freedom*, 8.

Chapter 4

1. Damon Mayrl and Freeden Oeur, "Religion and Higher Education: Current Knowledge and Directions for Future Research." *Journal for the Scientific Study of Religion* 48, no. 2 (2009): 260–75; Conrad Cherry, Betty A. DeBerg, and Amanda Porterfield, *Religion on Campus* (University of North Carolina Press, 2001); Melinda Lindquist Denton and Richard Denton, *Back-Pocket God: Religion and Spirituality in the Lives of Emerging Adults* (Oxford University Press, 2020).
2. Robert Bellah, "Flaws in the Protestant Code: Theological Roots of American Individualism," in *The Robert Bellah Reader*, eds. Robert N. Bellah and Steven M. Tipton (Duke University Press, 2006), 333–49.
3. John O'Brien, "Individualism as a Discursive Strategy of Action: Autonomy, Agency, and Reflexivity among Religious Americans." *Sociological Theory*, 33, no. 2 (2015): 173–99. https://doi.org/10.1177/07352751155883
4. Harold V. Hartley III, "How College Affects Students' Religious Faith and Practice: A Review of Research." *College Student Affairs Journal*, 23, no. 2 (2004): 111–29. https://www.proquest.com/scholarly-journals/how-college-affects-students-religious-faith/docview/224811506/se-2; Ernest Pascarella and Patrick Terenzini, *How College Affects Students: A Third Decade of Research* (Jossey-Bass, 2005); Cherry et al., *Religion on Campus;* Jeremy E. Uecker, Mark D. Regnerus, and Margaret L. Vaaler, "Losing My Religion: The Social Sources of Religious Decline in Early Adulthood," *Social Forces*, 85, no. 4 (2007): 1667–92,
5. Mayrl and Oeur, "Religion and Higher Education," 265.
6. Alexander W. Astin, Helen S. Astin, and Jennifer A. Lindholm, *Cultivating the Spirit: How College Can Enhance Students' Inner Lives* (Jossey-Bass, 2011).
7. Mayrl and Oeur, "Religion and Higher Education," 263.
8. Cherry et al., *Religion on Campus.*
9. Denton and Flory, *Back-Pocket God.*
10. Tim Clydesdale, *The First Year Out: Understanding American Teens after High School* (University of Chicago Press, 2007).
11. Damon Mayrl and Jeremy E. Uecker, "Higher Education and Religious Liberalization among Young Adults." *Social Forces*, 90, no. 1 (2011): 181–208.
12. Zaid Adhami, *Dilemmas of Authenticity: The American Muslim Crisis of Faith* (University of North Carolina Press, 2025).
13. Astin, Astin, and Lindholm, *Cultivating the Spirit*, 97.
14. Jenny Small, *Understanding College Students' Spiritual Identities: Different Faiths, Varied Worldviews* (Hampton Press, 2011).
15. O'Brien, "Individualism as a Discursive Strategy of Action."
16. Robert Bellah, Richard Madsen, William M. Sullivan, Ann Swidler, and Steven M. Tipton, *Habits of* (University of California Press, 2008).
17. Bellah et al., *Habits of the Heart*, 235.

18. See, for example: Joshua Foa Dienstag, "Reflections on Sheilaism." *The Hedgehog Review* 4, no. 1 (2002): 48–60; Melissa M. Wilcox, "When Sheila's a Lesbian: Religious Individualism among Lesbian, Gay, Transgender, and Bisexual Christians." *Sociology of Religion*, 63, no. 4 (2002):497–513, https://doi.org/10.2307/3712304; Bruce A. Greer and Wade Clark Roof. "'Desperately Seeking Sheila': Locating Religious Privatism in American Society." *Journal for the Scientific Study of Religion* 31, no. 3 (1992): 346–52. https://doi.org/10.2307/1387125.
19. Robert Wuthnow, *After Heaven: Spirituality in America since 1950s* (University of California Press, 1998).
20. Robert D. Putnam. *Bowling Alone: The Collapse and Revival of American Community* (Simon & Schuster, 2000).
21. Bellah, "Flaws in the Protestant Code."
22. Amanda Porterfield, *The Transformation of American Religion* (Oxford University Press, 2001).
23. O'Brien, "Individualism as a Discursive Strategy of Action."
24. O'Brien, "Individualism as a Discursive Strategy of Action," 174.
25. Ann Swidler, "Culture in Action: Symbols and Strategies." *American Sociological Review*, 51, no. 2 (1986): 273–86; Ann Swidler, *Talk of Love: How Culture Matters* (University of Chicago Press, 2001).
26. O'Brien, "Individualism as a Discursive Strategy of Action," 175.
27. O'Brien, "Individualism as a Discursive Strategy of Action," 194.
28. Mark Chaves, "Secularization as Declining Religious Authority." *Social Forces* 72, no. 3 (1994): 749–74. https://doi.org/10.2307/2579779
29. Porterfield, *The Transformation of American Religion*, 13.
30. O'Brien, "Individualism as a Discursive Strategy of Action."
31. O'Brien, "Individualism as a Discursive Strategy of Action."
32. Jeremy E. Uecker and Paul Froese, "Religious Individualism and Moral Progressivism: How Source of Religious Authority Is Related to Attitudes about Abortion, Same-Sex Marriage, Divorce, and Premarital Sex." *Politics and Religion*, 12 (2019): 283–316.
33. O'Brien, "Individualism as a Discursive Strategy of Action."
34. Saba Mahmood, *Politics of Piety* (Princeton University Press, 2005).
35. O'Brien, "Individualism as a Discursive Strategy of Action," 183.
36. O'Brien, "Individualism as a Discursive Strategy of Action," 182.
37. Astin, Astin, and Lindholm, *Cultivating the Spirit.*
38. O'Brien, "Individualism as a Discursive Strategy of Action".
39. David Vogel, "The Protestant Ethic and the Spirit of Environmentalism: The Cultural Roots of Green Politics and Policies," September 2001, Haas School of Business, https://faculty.haas.berkeley.edu/vogel/paperprot.pdf; Bellah, "Flaws in the Protestant Code."
40. *Shirk* is an Arabic term meaning "associating partners with God," implying that God is not One or Absolute in His Power.
41. This is a pseudonym.
42. Jacobsen and Jacobsen, 2012, *No Longer Invisible*, 28.
43. Riyad Ahmed Shahjahan, "Toward a Spiritual Praxis: The Role of Spirituality among Faculty of Color Teaching for Social Justice." *he Review of Higher Education*, 33, no. 4 (2010): 473–512.
44. Adhami, 2025; see Chapter 5, "Faith as Inheritance," 137–68.
45. Mayrl and Uecker, ""Higher Education and Religious Liberalization"; Wuthnow, *After Heaven*; Denton and Flory, *Back-Pocket God.*
46. Clydesdale, *The First Year Out*; Mayrl and Oeur, "Religion and Higher Education."
47. Mayrl and Oeur, "Religion and Higher Education."

48. Clydesdale, *The First Year Out.*
49. Cherry et al., *Religion on Campus.*
50. Christian Smith and Melinda Lundquist Denton, *Soul Searching: The Religious and Spiritual Lives of American Teenagers* (Oxford University Press, 2005).
51. Denton and Flory, *Back-Pocket God.*
52. Bellah et al., *Habits of the Heart.*
53. James Fowler, *Stages of Faith: The Psychology of Human Development and the Quest for Meaning* (Harper Collins, 1981).
54. Sharon Daloz Parks, "Faith Development," in *The Oxford Handbook of Religion and American Education*, eds. Michael D. Waggoner and Nathan C. Walker (Oxford University Press, 2018).
55. Parks, "Faith Development," 113.
56. Uecker and Froese, "Religious Individualism and Moral Progressivism," 309.
57. Mayrl and Uecker. 2011. "Higher Education and Religious Liberalization."
58. O'Brien, "Individualism as a Discursive Strategy of Action."

Chapter 5

1. Robert A. Dahl, *Democracy and Its Critics* (Yale University Press, 1989).
2. The quote is actually "Well, it's probably better to have him inside the tent pissing out, than outside pissing in." Johnson was quoted in the *New York Times* (October 31, 1971), making this remark about J. Edgar Hoover. See David Halberstam, *The Vantage Point Perspectives of the Presidency 1963–1969. By Lyndon Baines Johnson. Illustrated.* 636 pp. (Holt, Rinehart and Winston, *New York Times*, October 31, 1971). https://www.nytimes.com/1971/10/31/archives/the-vantage-point-perspectives-of-the-presidency-19631969-by-lyndon.html
3. Quoted in Robert Bellah. 2002. "The Protestant Structure of American Culture." *The Hedgehog Review* 4 (1): 16.
4. Amanda Porterfield, *The Transformation of American Religion* (Oxford University Press, 2001).
5. Ahmadi, Shafiqa, and Darnell Cole. 2025. "Combating Islamophobia on Campus: Racialization, Civil Rights, and the Fight for Muslim Belonging in Higher Education." *Change: The Magazine of Higher Learning* 57 (1): 4–10.
6. Nicholas Bowman and Jenny Small, "The Experiences and Spiritual Growth of Religiously Privileged and Religiously Marginalized College Students," in *Spirituality in College Students' Lives,* eds. Alyssa Rockenbach and Matthew J. Mayhew (Routledge 2012), 72.
7. Tracy Fessenden, *Culture and Redemption: Religion, the Secular, and American Literature* (Princeton University Press, 2007).

Bibliography

Abdul-Khabeer, Su'ad. *Muslim Cool: Race, Religion, and Hip Hop in the United States*. New York: New York University Press, 2016.

Adhami, Zaid. *Dilemmas of Authenticity: The American Muslim Crisis of Faith*. Chapel Hill: University of North Carolina Press, 2025.

Adhami, Zaid. *Faith with Doubt: American Muslims, Secularity, and the "Crisis of Faith."* PhD diss., Duke University, 2017.

Afzal, Ahmed. *Lone Star Muslims: Transnational Lives and the South Asian Experience in Texas*. New York: New York University Press, 2014.

Ahmadi, Shafiqa. "The Erosion of Civil Rights: Exploring the Effects of the Patriot Act on Muslims in American Higher Education." *Rutgers Race and the Law Review* 12, no. 1 (2011): 1–55. https://doi.org/10.1017/CBO9781107415324.004

Ahmadi, Shafiqa, and Darnell Cole. "Combating Islamophobia on Campus: Racialization, Civil Rights, and the Fight for Muslim Belonging in Higher Education." *Change: The Magazine of Higher Learning* 57, no. 1 (2025): 4–10. https://doi.org/10.1080/00091383.2025.2442878

Ahmadi, Shafiqa, and Darnell Cole, eds. *Islamophobia in Higher Education: Combatting Discrimination and Creating Understanding*. Sterling, VA: Stylus Publishing, 2020.

Ahmed, Abiya. "Muslim Student Associations in North America." *Oxford Research Encyclopedia of Religion*. April 16, 2025. Oxford University Press. https://doi.org/10.1093/acrefore/9780199340378.013.867

Ahmed, Sameera, Wahiba Abu-Ras, and Cynthia Arfken. "Prevalence of Risk Behaviors among U.S. Muslim College Students." *Journal of Muslim Mental Health* 8, no. 1 (2014): 1556–4908. https://doi.org/10.3998/jmmh.10381607.0008.101

Ali, Arshad Imtiaz. "A Threat Enfleshed: Muslim College Students Situate Their Identities Amidst Portrayals of Muslim Violence and Terror." *International Journal of Qualitative Studies in Education* 27, no.10 (2014): 1243–61. https://doi.org/10.1080/09518398.2013.820860

Ali, Saba Rasheed, and Elham Bagheri. "Practical Suggestions to Accommodate the Needs of Muslim Students." *New Directions for Student Services, Special Issue: Intersections of Religious Privilege* 125 (2009): 47–54. https://doi.org/10.1002/ss.307

Allen, Danielle. "How to Be a Confident Pluralist." Diversity Forum, University of Wisconsin-Madison, November 14, 2023. https://diversityforum.wisc.edu/session/danielle-allen-keynote/.

Alsultany, Evelyn. *Broken: The Failed Promise of Muslim Inclusion*. New York: NYU Press, 2022.

Antonio, Anthony Lising. "Diversity and the Influence of Friendship Groups in College." *The Review of Higher Education*, 25 no. 1 (2001): 63–89. https://dx.doi.org/10.1353/rhe.2001.0013

Arnett, Jeff Jensen. *Emerging Adulthood: The Winding Road from the Late Teens Through The Twenties*. New York: Oxford University Press, 2015.

Asad, Talal. *Formations of the Secular: Christianity, Islam, Modernity*. Stanford, CA. Stanford University Press, 2003.

Asad, Talal. *Genealogies of Religion: Discipline and Reasons of Power in Christianity and Islam*. Baltimore: Johns Hopkins University Press, 1993.

Astin, Alexander W., Helen S. Astin, and Jennifer A. Lindholm. *Cultivating the Spirit: How College Can Enhance Students' Inner Lives*. 1st ed. San Francisco: Jossey-Bass, 2010.

Astin, W. Alexander, Helen S. Astin, and Jennifer A. Lindholm. *Cultivating the Spirit: How College Can Enhance Students' Inner Lives*. San Francisco: Jossey-Bass, 2011.

Bellah, Robert N. "Civil Religion in America." *Daedalus* 96, no. 1 (1967): 1–21. http://www.jstor.org/stable/20027022.

Bellah, Robert. "Flaws in the Protestant Code: Theological Roots of American Individualism" in *The Robert Bellah Reader*, edited by R. N. Bellah and S. M. Tipton. Durham, NC: Duke University Press, 2006, 333–49.

Bellah, Robert. "Is There a Common American Culture?" in *The Robert Bellah Reader*, edited by R. N. Bellah and S. M. Tipton. Durham, NC: Duke University Press. 2006, 319–32.

Bellah, Robert. "The Protestant Structure of American Culture." *The Hedgehog Review* 4, no. 1 (2002): 16.

Bellah, Robert, Richard Madsen, William M. Sullivan, Ann Swidler, and Steven M. Tipton. *Habits of the Heart: Individualism and Commitment in American Life*. Berkeley: University of California Press, 1985.

Bender, Courtney, and Pamela E. Klassen, eds. *After Pluralism: Reimagining Religious Engagement*. New York: Columbia University Press, 2010.

Bender, Courtney, Wendy Cadge, Peggy Levitt, and David Smilde, eds. *Religion on the Edge: De-centering and Re-centering the Sociology of Religion*. Oxford, UK: Oxford University Press, 2013.

Berger, Peter. *The Sacred Canopy: Elements of a Sociological Theory of Religion*. New York: Anchor Books, 1967.

Beydoun, Khaled A. *American Islamophobia: Understanding the Roots and Rise of Fear*. Oakland, CA: University of California Press, 2018.

Binder, Amy J., and Kate Wood. *Becoming Right. How Campuses Shape Young Conservatives.* Princeton, NJ: Princeton University Press, 2013.

Blumenfeld, Warren. "Challenging Christian Hegemony and Christian Privilege in Academia." In *Handbook on Promoting Social Justice in Education*, edited by R. Papa. Cham: Springer, 2019. https://doi.org/10.1007/978-3-319-74078-2_113-1

Bowman, Nicholas, and Jenny Small. "The Experiences and Spiritual Growth of Religiously Privileged and Religiously Marginalized College Students." In *Spirituality in College Students' Lives*, edited by Alyssa Rockenbach and Matthew J. Mayhew, 71–85. New York and London: Routledge, 2012.

Brest, Paul, and Emily J. Levine. "D.E.I. Is Not Working on College Campuses. We Need a New Approach." *New York Times*, August 30, 2024. https://www.nytimes.com/2024/08/30/opinion/college-dei-programs-diversity.html.

Brinkmann, Svend, and Kvale Steinar. *InterViews: Learning the Craft of Qualitative Research Interviewing.* Los Angeles: SAGE Publications, 2015.

Brown, Jonathan A.C. *Misquoting Muhammad: The Challenge and Choices of Interpreting the Prophet's Legacy.* London: Oneworld Publications, 2014

Bryant, Alyssa. "Exploring Religious Pluralism in Higher Education: Non-Majority Religious Perspectives among Entering First-Year Students." *Religion and Education* 33, no. 1 (2006): 1–25. https://doi.org/10.1080/15507394.2006.1001236

Bryant, Alyssa. "The Impact of Campus Context, College Encounters, and Religious/Spiritual Struggle on Ecumenical Worldview Development." *Research in Higher Education* 52 (2011): 441–459. https://doi.org/10.1007/s11162-010-9205-0

Bryant, Alyssa N., Keith Wickliffe, Matthew J. Mayhew, and Laurie B. Behringer. "Developing an Assessment of College Students' Spiritual Experiences: The Collegiate Religious and Spiritual Climate Survey." *Journal of College and Character* 10, no. 6 (2009). https://doi.org/10.2202/1940-1639.1452

Burke, Lilah. "DEI at Public Colleges, Medical Schools Comes under Congressional Attack." *Higher Ed Dive*, March 7, 2024. https://www.highereddive.com/news/house-committee-hearing-dei-college-campuses/709684/.

Cadge, Wendy, and Mary Ellen Konieczny. "'Hidden in Plain Sight': The Significance of Religion and Spirituality in Secular Organizations." *Sociology of Religion* 75, no. 4 (2014): 551–63. https://doi.org/10.1093/socrel/sru043.

Canell, Fenella. "The Anthropology of Secularism." *Annual Review of Anthropology* 39 (2010): 85–100. https://doi.org/10.1146/annurev.anthro.012809.105039

Casanova, José. *Public Religions in the Modern World.* Chicago: University of Chicago Press, 1994.

Casanova, Jose. "The Secular and Secularisms." *Social Research* 76, no. 4 (2009): 1049–66. http://www.jstor.org/stable/40972201

Chan-Malik, Sylvia. *Being Muslim: A Cultural History of Women of Color.* New York: New York University Press, 2018.

Chaudhury, Sadia, and Lisa Miller. "Religious Identity Formation among Bangladeshi American Muslim Adolescents." *Journal of Adolescent Research, 23*, no. 4 (2008): 383–410. https://doi.org/10.1177/0743558407309277

Chaves, Mark. "Secularization as Declining Religious Authority." *Social Forces* 72, no. 3 (1994): 749–74. https://doi.org/10.2307/2579779.

Cherry, Conrad, Betty A. DeBerg, and Amanda Porterfield. *Religion on Campus.* Chapel Hill: University of North Carolina Press, 2001.

Cole, Darnell, and Shafiqa Ahmadi. "Perspectives and Experiences of Muslim Women Who Veil on College Campuses." *Journal of College Student Development* 44, no. 1 (2003): 47–66. https://doi.org/10.1353/csd.2003.0002

Cole, Darnell, and Shafiqa Ahmadi. "Reconsidering Campus Diversity: An Examination of Muslim Students' Experiences." *The Journal of Higher Education* 81, no. 2 (2010): 121–39. https://doi.org/10.1080/00221546.2010.11779045

Currier, Cora. "Muslim Students Speak Out Against FBI Informant Plan Exposed by the Intercept," October 17, 2016. *The Intercept.* https://theintercept.com/2016/10/17/muslim-students-speak-out-against-fbi-informant-plan-exposed-by-the-intercept/

Cuyjet, Michal J., Mary F. Howard-Hamilton, and Diane L. Cooper, eds. *Multiculturalism on Campus: Theories, Models and Practices for Understanding Diversity and Creating Inclusion.* Sterling, VA: Stylus Publishing, 2011.

Dahl, Robert A. *Democracy and Iits Critics.* New Haven: Yale University Press, 1989.

Denton, Melinda Lindquist, and Richard Flory. *Back-Pocket God: Religion and Spirituality in the Lives of Emerging Adults.* New York: Oxford University Press, 2020.

Denton, Melinda Lindquist, and Christian Smith. *Soul Searching: The Religious and Spiritual Lives of American Teenagers.* New York: Oxford University Press, 2005.

Dienstag, Joshua Foa. "Reflections on Sheilaism." *The Hedgehog Review* 4, no. 1 (2002): 48.

"The Dismantling of DEI." 2024. *Chronicle of Higher Education.* https://www.chronicle.com/package/the-assault-on-dei.

"Diversity, Equity, and Inclusion Initiatives with Brian Lowery, Iván Marinovic, and Eboo Patel." *Democracy and Disagreement.* 2024. https://humsci.stanford.edu/events/2025-02-11/diversity-equity-and-inclusion-initiatives-brian-lowery-ivan-marinovic-and-eboo.

Eck, Diana. "Pluralism: Problems and Promise." In *The Oxford Handbook of Religion and American Education*, edited by Michael D. Waggoner and Nathan C. Walker, 9. New York: Oxford University Press, 2018.

Eck, Diana. "Prospects for Pluralism: Voice and Vision in the Study of Religion." *Journal of the American Academy of Religion* 75, no. 4 (2007): 743–76. http://www.jstor.org/stable/40005962.

Eck, Diana, and Brendan Randall. "Pluralism in Religion and American Education." In *The Oxford Handbook of Religion and American Education*, edited by Michael D. Waggoner and Nathan C. Walker, 9. New York: Oxford University Press, 2018.

Edwards, Sachi, Jenny L. Small, Matthew R. Sayers, and Simran Kaur-Colbert. "'One More Thing': Clarifying the Evidence Around Christian Privilege in Higher Education." *Religion & Education* 50, no. 4 (2023): 246–56. https://doi.org/10.1080/15507394.2023.2271818

Emerson, Robert M., Rachel I. Fretz, and Linda L. Shaw. *Writing Ethnographic Fieldnotes*. Chicago: University of Chicago Press, 2011.

Fawzi, Salua. Experiencing Islam in America: Muslim Students Associations. Unpublished doctoral dissertation, McGill University, 2019.

Fessenden, Tracy. *Culture and Redemption: Religion, the Secular, and American Literature*. Princeton, NJ: Princeton University Press, 2007.

Geertz, Clifford. *Local Knowledge: Further Essays in Interpretive Anthropology*. New York: Basic Books, 2008.

GhaneaBassiri, Kambiz. *A History of Islam in America: From the New World to the New World Order*. New York: Cambridge University Press, 2010.

Gilliat-Ray, Sophie. *Religion in Higher Education: The Politics of the Multi-Faith Campus*. New York: Routledge, 2019.

Glanzer, Perry L. "Recognizing Christian Complexity and Secular Privilege in Higher Education: A Response to Recent Christian Privilege Arguments." *Religion & Education* 49, no. 2 (2022): 119–37. https://doi.org/10.1080/15507394.2022.2051973.

Glanzer, Perry L., and Jessica Martin. "Recognizing the 'Both-And' Instead of Promulgating the 'Either-Or': A Critical Response to Critical Religion Scholars." *Religion & Education* 50, no. 4 (2023): 232–45. https://doi.org/10.1080/15507394.2023.2245942.

Gorski, Philip, David Kyuman Kim, John Tropey and Jonathan VanAnterwerpen. *The Post-Secular in Question*. New York: New York University Press, 2012.

Grewal, Zareena. *Islam Is a Foreign Country: American Muslims and the Global Crisis of Authority*. New York: New York University Press, 2014.

Hammer, Juliane. *American Muslim Women, Religious Authority, and Activism: More than a Prayer*. Austin: University of Texas Press, 2012.

Harper, Shaun, et al. "Truths about DEI on College Campuses." *USC Race and Equity Center*, March 2024. https://race.usc.edu/wp-content/uploads/2024/03/Harper-and-Associates-DEI-Truths-Report.pdf.

Hart, D.G. *The University Gets Religion: Religious Studies in American Higher Education*. Baltimore. MD: Johns Hopkins University Press, 1999.

Hartley, Harold V., III. "How College Affects Students' Religious Faith and Practice: A Review of Research." *College Student Affairs Journal* 23, no. 2 (2004): 111–29. https://eric.ed.gov/?id=EJ956982

Herberg, Will. *Protestant—Catholic—Jew: An Essay in American Religious Sociology*. Chicago: University of Chicago Press, 1983.

Herzig, Benjamin, Gargi Roysircar, Kristin Kosyluk, and Patrick Corrigan. "American Muslim College Students: The Impact of Religiousness and Stigma on Active Coping." *Journal of Muslim Mental Health* 7, no. 1 (2013): 33–42. http://hdl.handle.net/2027/spo.10381607.0007.103

Hicks, Rosemary R. "Religious Pluralism, Secularism, and Interfaith Endeavors." In *The Cambridge Companion to American Islam*, edited by Juliane Hammer and Omid Safi, 156–69. Cambridge Companions to Religion. Cambridge: Cambridge University Press, 2013.

Hofstadter Richard, and Walter P. Metzger. *The Development of Academic Freedom in the United States*. New York: Columbia University Press, 1955.

Howell, Sally. "Laying the Groundwork for American Muslim Histories: 1865–1965. In *The Cambridge Companion to American Islam*, edited by Juliane Hmmer and Omid Safi, 45–64. New York: Cambridge University Press, 2013.

Hulsether, Linda. "Grammar of Racism: Religious Pluralism and the Birth of Interdisciplines." *Journal of the American Academy of Religion* 86, no. 1 (2017): 1–41. https://doi.org/10.1093/jaarel/lfx049

Hulsether, Lucia. "Out of Incorporation, Pluralism." *Journal of Interreligious Studies* 17 (2015): 45–53. https://irstudies.org/index.php/jirs/article/view/307/291

Hutchinson, William. *Religious Pluralism in America: The Contentious History of an American Ideal*. New Haven, CT: Yale University Press, 2004.

Imhoff, Sarah. "The Creation Story, or How We Learned to Stop Worrying and Love *Schempp*." *Journal of the American Academy of Religion* 84, no. 2 (2016): 466–97. https://doi.org/10.1093/jaarel/lfv060

Inazu, John. "Hope Without a Common Good." In *Out of Many Faiths*, edited by Eboo Patel, 148–67. Princeton University Press, 2018.

Jackson, Sherman. *Islam and the Blackamerican*: Looking toward the Third Resurrection. New York: Oxford University Press, 2005.

Jacobsen, Douglass, and Rhonda Jacobsen, eds. *The American University in a Postsecular Age*. New York: Oxford University Press, 2008.

Jacobsen, Rhonda Hustedt, and Douglas Jacobsen. *No Longer Invisible: Religion in University Education*. New York: Oxford University Press, 2012.

Jakobsen, Janet, and Ann Pellegrini, eds. *Secularisms*. Durham, NC: Duke University Press, 2008.

Johnson, Karla, and Peter Laurence. "Multi-Faith Religious Spaces on College and University Campuses." *Religion and Education* 39, no. 1 (2012): 48–63. https://doi.org/10.1080/15507394.2012.648579

Jones, Robert P. "The Challenge of Pluralism after the End of White Christian America." In *Out of Many Faiths*, edited by Eboo Patel, 113–32. Princeton. NJ: Princeton University Press, 2018.

Karlin-Neumann, Patricia, and Joanne Sanders. "Bringing Faith to Campus: Religious and Spiritual Space, Time, and Practice at Stanford University." *Journal of College and Character* 14, no. 2 (2013): 125–32. https://doi.org/10.1515/jcc-2013-0017

Khalil, Nancy. "How Campus Protests Exposed the Flaws in Higher Education Diversity Initiatives." *Middle East Eye*, September 2, 2024. https://www.middleeasteye.net/opinion/how-campus-protests-exposed-flaws-university-diversity-initiatives.

Khyati, Joshi. *White Christian Privilege: The Illusion of Religious Equality in America.* New York: New York University Press, 2020.

Kocet, M. M., and D. L. Stewart. "The Role of Student Affairs in Promoting Religious and Secular Pluralism and Interfaith Cooperation." *Journal of College and Character* 12 no. 1 (2011): 1–10. https://doi.org/10.2202/1940-1639.1762

Labaree, David. *A Perfect Mess: The Unlikely Ascendancy of American Higher Education.* Chicago, University of Chicago Press, 2017.

Lajevardi, Nazita, and Kassra A. R. Oskooii. "Old-Fashioned Racism, Contemporary Islamophobia, and the Isolation of Muslim Americans in the Age of Trump." *Journal of Race, Ethnicity, and Politics* 3 (2018): 112–52. https://doi.org/10.1017/rep.2017.37

Lane, A. Glenn. "It's Time to Turn the Page on DEI." *Inside Higher Ed*, March 11, 2025. https://www.insidehighered.com/opinion/views/2025/03/11/its-time-turn-page-dei-opinion.

Lizardo, Omar. "Improving Cultural Analysis: Considering Personal Culture in Its Declarative and Nondeclarative Modes." *American Sociological Review* 82, no. 1 (2017): 88–115. https://doi.org/10.1177/0003122416675175

Lloyd, Vincent W. "Introduction: Managing Race, Managing Religion." In – *Race and Secularism in America*, edited by Jonathan S. Kahn and Vincent W. Lloyd, 1–18. New York: Columbia University Press, 2016.

Love, Erik. *Islamophobia and Racism in America.* New York: New York University Press, 2017.

Mahmood, Saba. *Politics of Piety: The Islamic Revival and the Feminist Subject.* Princeton, NJ: Princeton University Press, 2005.

Mahmood, Saba. *Religious Difference in a Secular Age: A Minority Report.* Princeton, NJ: Princeton University Press, 2015.

Maples, Gordon, Leah Rediger, and Jenny L. Small. "Privilege as Policy? An Analysis of Student Religious Accommodation Policies in Higher Education." *Journal of College and Character* 22, no. 4 (2021): 272–90. https://doi.org/10.1080/2194587X.2021.1977151

Marsden, George. *The Soul of the American University: From Protestant Establishment to Established Nonbelief.* New York: Oxford University Press, 1994.

Marsden, George. *The Soul of the American University Revisited: From Protestant to Postsecular*. New York: Oxford University Press, 2021.

Marty, Martin. *The Protestant Voice in American Pluralism*. Athens: University of Georgia Press, 2004.

Masuzawa, Tomoko. *The Invention of World Religions*. Chicago: University of Chicago Press, 2005.

Mayhew, Matthew J., Nicholas A. Bowman, and Alyssa Bryant Rockenbach. "Silencing Whom? Linking Campus Climates for Religious, Spiritual, and Worldview Diversity to Student Worldviews." *The Journal of Higher Education* 85, no. 2 (2014): 219–45. https://doi.org/10.1080/00221546.2014.11777325

Mayrl, Damon, and Jeremy E. Uecker. "Higher Education and Religious Liberalization among Young Adults." *Social Forces* 90, no. 1 (2011): 181–208. https://doi.org/10.1093/sf/90.1.181

Mayrl, Damon, and Freeden Oeur. "Religion and Higher Education: Current Knowledge and Directions for Future Research." *Journal for the Scientific Study of Religion* 48, no. (2009): 260–75. https://doi.org/10.1111/j.1468-5906.2009.01446.x

McCreary, Charles, and Jeffrey Wheatley. "The Protestant Secular in the Study of American Religion: Reappraisal and Suggestions." *Religion* 47, no. 2 (2017): 256–76. https://doi.org/10.1080/0048721X.2016.1244124

McCutcheon, Russell. "'Just Follow the Money: The Cold War, The Humanistic Study of Religion, and the Fallacy of Insufficient Cynicism." *Culture and Religion* 5, no. 1 (2004): 41–69. https://doi.org/10.1080/0143830042000200355

McCutcheon, Russell. *Manufacturing Religion: The Discourse on sui generis Religion and the Politics of Nostalgia*. New York: Oxford University Press. 1997.

Mir, Shabana. *Muslim American Women on Campus: Undergraduate Life and Identity*. Chapel Hill: University of North Carolina Press, 2014.

Mir, Shabana. "Not Too "College-Like," Not Too Normal: American Muslim Undergraduate Women's Gendered Discourses." *Anthropology and Education Quarterly* 40, no. 3 (2009): 237–56. http://www.jstor.org/stable/25602226.

Modern, John. *Secularism in Antebellum America*. Chicago: University of Chicago Press, 2011.

Mogahed, Dalia. "Winning Muslim Votes: A Policy Priority Analysis in Swing States." Institute of Social Policy and Understanding (ISPU), September 17, 2024. https://ispu.org/winning-muslim-votes-1/.

Morales, Harold. *Latino and Muslim in America: Race, Religion, and the Making of a New Minority*. New York: Oxford University Press, 2018.

Muir, Scott. "The Adhan Controversy in Historical Perspective: Interpenetrating Protestant, Secular, and Pluralist Paradigms at Duke

University, 1839–2016." *Journal of Religion and Society* 19 (2017): 1–22. http://hdl.handle.net/10504/113357

Mubarak, Hadia. "How Muslim Students Negotiate Their Religious Identity and Practices in an Undergraduate Setting." *The Religious Engagement of American Undergraduates, Social Science Research Council*, 8 May 2007, www.researchgate.net/publication/251290330_How_Muslim_Students_Negotiate_their_Religious_Identity_and_Practices_in_an_Undergraduate_Setting

Nash, Robert. *Religious Pluralism in the Academy: Opening the Dialogue.* New York: Peter Lang Publishing, 2011.

Nasir, Nailah, and Jamil Al-Amin. "Creating Identity-Safe Spaces on College Campuses for Muslim Students." *Change: The Magazine of Higher Learning* 38, no. 2 (2006): 22–27. https://doi.org/10.3200/CHNG.38.2.22-27

Nongbri, Brent. *Before Religion: A History of a Modern Concept.* New Haven, CT: Yale University Press. 2013.

Nord, Warren. *Does God Make a Difference? Taking Religion Seriously in Our Schools and Universities.* New York: Oxford University Press, 2010.

O'Brien, John. "Individualism as a Discursive Strategy of Action: Autonomy, Agency, and Reflexivity among Religious Americans." *Sociological Theory* 33, no. 2 (2015): 173–99. https://doi.org/10.1177/0735275115588353

Parks, Sharon. *Big Questions, Worthy Dreams: Mentoring Young Adults in Their Search for Meaning, Purpose, and Faith.* San Francisco: John Wiley & Sons, 2000.

Parks, Sharon. *The Critical Years: The Young Adult Search for a Faith to Live By.* San Francisco: Harper & Row, 1986.

Parks, Sharon Daloz. "Faith Development." In *The Oxford Handbook of Religion and American Education*, edited by Michael D. Waggoner and Nathan C. Walker, 113–27. New York: Oxford University Press, 2018.

Patel, Eboo. *Out of Many Faiths: Religious Diversity and the American Promise.* Princeton, NJ: Princeton University Press, 2018.

Patel, Eboo. "The Civic Relevance of Interfaith Cooperation for Colleges and Universities." *From the Guest Editors of Special Issue on Interfaith Cooperation Journal of College & Character* 12, no. 1 (2011). https://doi.org/10.2202/1940-1639.1764

Patel, Eboo, and Benjamin P. Correia-Harker. "Bonding and Bridging: An Equilibrium That Matters for Engaging Religious Diversity in a Pluralistic Society." *Journal of College and Character* 21, no. 1 (2020): 42–48. https://doi.org/10.1080/2194587x.2019.1696833

Peek, Lori. "Becoming Muslim: The Development of a Religious Identity." *Sociology of Religion* 66, no. 3 (2005): 215–42. http://www.jstor.org/stable/4153097

Porterfield, Amanda. "Religious Pluralism, the Study of Religion, and Postsecular Culture." In *The American University in a Postsecular Age*, edited by Douglas Jacobsen and Rhonda Jacobsen, 196. New York: Oxford University Press, 2008.

Porterfield, Amanda. *The Transformation of American Religion.* New York: Oxford University Press, 2001.

Putnam, Robert D. *Bowling Alone: The Collapse and Revival of American Community.* New York: Simon & Schuster, 2000.

Rabia, Kamal. "American Muslim Youth Movements. *The Oxford Handbook of American Islam.* New York: Oxford University Press, 2014.

Reuben, Julie A. *The Making of the Modern University.* Chicago: University of Chicago Press, 1996.

Rinaldo, Rachel, and Jeffrey Guhin. "How and Why Interviews Work: Ethnographic Interviews and Meso-Level Public Culture." *Sociological Methods and Research* 51, no. 1(2019): 34–67. https://doi.org/10.1177/0049124119882471

Roald, Anne Sofie. "Who Are the Muslims?: Questions of Identity, Gender and Culture in Research Methodologies." In *Gender, Religion & Diversity: Cross-Cultural Perspectives*, edited by U. King and T. Beattie, 179–89. London: Continuum, 2004.

Rockenbach, Alyssa Bryant, and Matthew Mayhew. *Spirituality in College Students' Lives: Translating Research into Practice.* New York: Routledge, 2013.

Rockenbach, Alyssa, Matthew J. Mayhew, Shauna Morin, Rebecca E. Crandall, and Ben Selznick. "Fostering the Pluralism Orientation of College Students through Interfaith Co-curricular Engagement." *The Review of Higher Education* 39, no. 1 (2015): 25–58, https://dx.doi.org/10.1353/rhe.2015.0040.

Roof, Wade Clark. *Spiritual Marketplace: Baby Boomers and the Remaking of American Religion.* Princeton, NJ: Princeton University Press, 1999.

Rosa, Jonathan, and Yarimar Bonilla. "Deprovincializing Trump, Decolonizing Diversity, and Unsettling Anthropology." *American Ethnologist* 44, no. 2 (2017): 201–8. https://doi.org/10.1111/amet.12468

Rudolph, Fredrick. *The American College and University: A History.* Georgia: University of Georgia Press, 1962.

Schmaulzbauer, John, and Kathleen Mahoney. *The Resilience of Religion in American Education.* Dallas, TX: Baylor University Press, 2018.

Schmidt, Garbi. *Islam in Urban America: Sunni Muslims in Chicago.* Philadelphia: Temple University Press, 2004.

Seggie, Fatma and Gretchen Sanford. "Perceptions of female Muslim Students Who Veil: Campus Religious Climate." *Race Ethnicity and Education* 13, no. 1 (2010): 59–82. https://doi.org/10.1080/13613320903549701

Seifert, Tricia. "Understanding Christian Privilege: Managing the Tensions of Spiritual Plurality." *About Campus: Enriching the Student Learning Experience* 12, no. 2 (2007): 10–17. https://doi.org/10.1002/abc.206

Shahjahan, Riyad Ahmed. "Toward a Spiritual Praxis: The Role of Spirituality among Faculty of Color Teaching for Social Justice." *The Review of Higher Education* 33, no. 4 (2010): 473–512. https://dx.doi.org/10.1353/rhe.0.0166

Shammas, D. "Underreporting Discrimination among Arab American and Muslim American Community College Students: Using Focus Groups to Unravel the Ambiguities within the Survey Data." *Journal of Mixed Methods Research* 11, no. 1 (2017): 99–123. https://doi.org/10.1177/1558689815599467

Shammas, D. S. "Post-9/11 Arab and Muslim American Community College Students: Ethno-religious Enclaves and Perceived Discrimination." *Community College Journal of Research and Practice* 33 no. 3–4 (2009): 283–308. https://doi.org/10.1080/10668920802580507

Small, Jenny. *Critical Religious Pluralism in Higher Education.* New York: Routledge, 2020.

Small, Jenny L. *Understanding College Students' Spiritual Identities: Different Faiths, Varied Worldviews.* New York: Hampton Press, 2011.

Small, Jenny, and Nicholas Bowman. "Religious Affiliation and College Student Development: A Literature Review and Synthesis." *Religion and Education* 39, no. 1 (2012): 64–75. https://doi.org/10.1080/15507394.2012.648586

Small, Jenny L., and Nicholas A. Bowman. "Religious Commitment, Skepticism, and Struggle mong U.S. College Students: The Impact of Majority/Minority Religious Affiliation and Institutional Type." *Journal for the Scientific Study of Religion* 50, no. 1 (2011): 154–74. https://doi.org/10.1111/j.1468-5906.2010.01557.x.

Small, Jenny L., Sachi Edwards, Matthew R. Sayers, Renee L. Bowling, Julia R. Collett, Simran Kaur-Colbert, and J. Cody Nielsen. "Recognizing Christian Hegemony as Broader than Christian Privilege: Critical Religion Scholars Respond to Glanzer (2022)." *Religion & Education* 49, no. 4 (2022): 355–73. doi:10.1080/15507394.2022.2139996

Smith, Christian. *Souls in Transition: The Religious and Spiritual Lives of Emerging Adults.* New York: Oxford University Press, 2009.

Smith, Christian. *The Secular Revolution: Power, Interests, and Conflict in the Secularization of American Public Life.* BerkEley: University of California Press, 2003.

Smith, Christian, and Melinda Lundquist Denton. *Soul Searching: The Religious and Spiritual Lives of American Teenagers.* New York: Oxford University Press, 2005.

Smith, Jonathan Z. "Religion, Religions, Religious." In *Critical Terms for Religious Studies*, edited by Mark Taylor, 269–84. Chicago: University of Chicago Press, 1998.

Sommerville, John. *The Decline of the Secular University.* New York: Oxford University Press, 2006.

Speck, Bruce W. "Respect for Religious Differences: The Case of Muslim Students." *New Directions for Teaching and Learning*, 70 (1997): 39–46. https://doi.org/10.1002/tl.7004

Speers, Samuel. "The Secular Thesis Revisited: Religious Life on the Secular College Campus Today." *Journal of College and Character* 10, no. 1 (2008). https://doi.org/10.2202/1940-1639.1056

Spradley, James. *The Ethnographic Interview*. Belmont, CA: Wadsworth, 1979.

Stahl, Ronit. "A Jewish America and a Protestant Civil Religion: Will Herberg, Robert Bellah, and Mid-Twentieth Century American Religion." *Religions* 6 (2015): 434–50. https://doi:10.3390/rel6020434.

Stubbs, Benjamin, and Margaret Sallee. "Muslim, Too: Navigating Multiple Identities at an American University." *Equity and Excellence in Education* 46, no. 4 (2013): 451–67. https://doi.org/10.1080/10665684.2013.838129

Sullivan, Winnifred. *The Impossibility of Religious Freedom*, 2nd ed. Princeton: Princeton University Press. 2018.

Swidler, Ann. "Culture in Action: Symbols and Strategies." *American Sociological Review* 51, no. 2 (1986): 273–86. https://doi.org/10.2307/2095521.

Taylor, Charles. *A Secular Age*. Cambridge, MA: Harvard University Press, 2007.

Thelin, John R. *A History of American Higher Education*. Baltimore: Johns Hopkins University Press, 2004.

Uecker, Jeremy E., and Paul Froese. "Religious Individualism and Moral Progressivism: How Source of Religious Authority Is Related to Attitudes About Abortion, Same-Sex Marriage, Divorce, and Premarital Sex." *Politics and Religion* 12, no. 2 (2019): 283–316. https://doi.org/10.1017/S1755048318000792

Vogel, David. "The Protestant Ethic and the Spirit of Environmentalism: The Cultural Roots of Green Politics and Policies." *UC Berkeley Haas School of Business*, 2001. https://faculty.haas.berkeley.edu/vogel/paperprot.pdf

Wadud, Amina. *Inside the Gender Jihad: Women's Reform in Islam*. Oxford: Oneworld, 2006.

Waggoner, Michael. *Sacred and Secular Tensions in Higher Education*. New York: Routledge, 2011.

Waggoner, Michael D., and Nathan C. Walker, eds. *The Oxford Handbook of Religion and American Education*. New York: Oxford University Press, 2018.

Warikoo, Natasha. *The Diversity Bargain: and Other Dilemmas of Race, Admissions, and Meritocracy at Elite Universities*. Chicago: University of Chicago Press, 2016.

Warner, Michael. "Was Antebellum America Secular?" *The Immanent Frame*, October 2, 2012. https://tif.ssrc.org/2012/10/02/was-antebellum-america-secular/.

Warner, Michael, Jonathan VanAntwerpen, and Craig Calhoun, eds. *Varieties of Secularism in a Secular Age*. Cambridge, MA: Harvard University Press, 2010.

Weisenfeld, Judith. *New World A-Coming: Black Religion and Racial Identity during the Great Migration*. New York: New York University Press, 2017.

Wilcox, Melissa M. "When Sheila's a Lesbian: Religious Individualism among Lesbian, Gay, Transgender, and Bisexual Christians." *Sociology of Religion* 63, no. 4 (2002): 497–513. https://doi.org/10.2307/3712304.

Williams, Rhys, and Gira Vashi. "'Hijab and American Muslim Women: Creating the Space for Autonomous Selves." *Sociology of Religion* 68, no. 3 (2007): 269–87. https://www.jstor.org/stable/20453164

Wolterstorff, Nicholas. *Religion in the University*. New Haven, CT: Yale University Press, 2019.

Wuthnow, Robert. *After Heaven: Spirituality in America since 1950s*. Berkeley: University of California Press, 1999.

Index

For the benefit of digital users, indexed terms that span two pages (e.g., 52–53) may, on occasion, appear on only one of those pages.